STAND PRICE
$5.00
03/24

W9-DFT-182

GREAT SOUPS

ORLA BRODERICK

PHOTOGRAPHS BY
ROBIN MATTHEWS

RIZZOLI
NEW YORK

CONTENTS

A WELL-STOCKED KITCHEN

You will find most of the ingredients I use regularly are fairly straightforward, with a few little luxuries thrown in. It is amazing how many unexpected situations you can take in your stride if your kitchen is well stocked. Obviously, you don't need to have all of the following ingredients all of the time, but you'll find that if you cook regularly, none of them will go to waste.

Keep ingredients in the pantry in small quantities and make an effort to use them before their expiration date.

Always use the best quality you can afford—I buy organic or free-range produce whenever possible. Try to buy vegetables when they are in season; not only will they be the freshest and tastiest, but they will save you money as well.

IN THE PANTRY

BAY LEAVES

CANS OF VARIOUS BEANS AND CHICKPEAS

BOTTLES OF SAUCES AND PASTES, SUCH AS CHILI AND GARLIC SAUCE OR HARISSA; SOY SAUCE; HOT-PEPPER SAUCE; THAI FISH SAUCE (*NAM PLA*); WORCESTERSHIRE SAUCE

CHINESE NOODLES

PLAIN FLOUR

HONEY

BOTTLES OF EXTRA-VIRGIN OLIVE OIL, SUNFLOWER OIL, AND SESAME OIL

FINE AND COARSE SEA SALT

GROUND SPICES, SUCH AS CURRY POWDER, PAPRIKA, AND TURMERIC

WHOLE SPICES, SUCH AS SMALL DRIED CHILIES; CORIANDER AND CUMIN SEEDS; NUTMEG; BLACK AND WHITE PEPPERCORNS; STAR ANISE

A SELECTION OF BOUILLON CUBES

A SELECTION OF SUGARS, INCLUDING LIGHT BROWN AND SUPERFINE

CANS OF CRUSHED TOMATOES AND TUBES OR JARS OF TOMATO PASTE

TORTILLA CHIPS

IN THE REFRIGERATOR

BUTTER

CHEDDAR AND PARMESAN CHEESES

CRÈME FRAÎCHE OR SOUR CREAM

HEAVY CREAM

SCALLIONS

BOTTLE OF DRY WHITE WINE

PLAIN YOGURT

IN THE FREEZER

BREAD

PEAS

PUFF PASTRY DOUGH

SPINACH

CARTONS OF STORE-BOUGHT AND HOMEMADE (IF YOU'RE REALLY ORGANIZED!) CHICKEN AND VEGETABLE STOCKS

WHITE CRAB MEAT

IN THE VEGETABLE BASKET

CARROTS

CELERY

FRESH CHILIES

GARLIC

GINGERROOT

LEEKS

LEMONS

LIMES

ONIONS

RED BELL PEPPERS

POTATOES

SHALLOTS

ON THE WINDOW SILL

I would be lost without the selection of fresh herbs I have growing so conveniently on my window sill. I also always keep my tomatoes on the window sill, as it helps them continue to ripen and develop flavor. The selection of herbs I recommend are:

BASIL	FLAT-LEAF PARSLEY
CHERVIL	SAGE
CHIVES	TARRAGON
MINT	THYME

EQUIPMENT

With the exception of a good sharp knife, a decent chopping board, and a large, deep saucepan (preferably with a tight-fitting lid),

very little specialty equipment is necessary to prepare and cook the soups from this book. However, the following items

definitely have their uses (and I occasionally call for a food processor or a hand-held blender to purée soups):

FOOD PROCESSOR
I often purée soups and a food processor does this perfectly, even if you do have to do it in batches. If you have the space, give your food processor a permanent place on your countertop, because not only does it save time but you will use it more often.

HAND-HELD BLENDER
I think this is one of the most practical pieces of electrical equipment on the market today. I use it all the time for puréeing soups. Just hold the blender directly in the pan, which also saves on the dish washing! Most of the brands also come with a detachable bowl, which is the perfect size for blending small amounts of ingredients, such as when making pestos.

STRAINER
A good-quality, fine sieve should last you a lifetime. It allows you to strain your finished soups for a much smoother, velvety texture. It simply removes all of the tough, fibrous pieces without taking away any of the flavor. Just use a little elbow grease and the back of a wooden spoon to work the ingredients through the fine mesh. Occasionally I recommend passing clear, consommé-style soups or any type of shellfish cooking liquid through a cheesecloth-lined strainer, which removes even finer particles.

VEGETABLE MILL
This can be a most useful gadget in the art of soup making. It is actually a sophisticated strainer with a built-in masher that has three different sizes of metal disks for varying degrees of puréeing. It also normally comes with folding feet that secure it over your pan or bowl and help to hold it steady. Vegetable mills are relatively inexpensive and there is no danger of them breaking down, but the downside is that they can be difficult to clean.

LADLE
A good-sized ladle is invaluable when you need to transfer soup into a food processor in batches. It allows you to control the amount of solids and liquid that go into each batch. It is also useful when serving soup as it helps you judge the right quantity per person.

DRAINING/SLOTTED SPOON
This is useful for lifting cooked fish and shellfish or dumplings and wontons out of hot liquids to prevent overcooking. It also makes it easier to remove a bouquet garni or bay leaf from the soup.

SKIMMER
Use this to take off any foam and excess fat that rises to the surface of your stockpot, resulting in a clearer finished broth. The advantage of using a skimmer is that it takes only the bare amount and allows the liquid to drain back into the pan.

THE RECIPES

THE BASICS

The recipes in this section are for garnishes and other simple ideas to improve the flavor of your soups,

such as making your own stock. Most are a last-minute optional extra to add a texture variation and something

pleasing to the eye. They also give you infinite scope to vary and personalize the recipes.

CHICKEN STOCK

It is important to taste stock regularly while it cooks because it will eventually reach a point where the flavor stops improving. This happens after 2 to 3 hours. Makes about 3¾ cups.

1 chicken carcass with scraps of skin   *2 leeks, chopped*
   and the giblets, if available   *1 bay leaf*
1 onion, unpeeled and quartered   *1 fresh thyme sprig*
2 celery sticks, chopped   *½ ounce fresh parsley or tarragon stems*
1 large carrot, chopped   *6 black peppercorns*

Place all the ingredients in a large saucepan. Cover with about 2 quarts cold water and bring to a boil, skimming off any fat or foam.

Reduce the heat and simmer for 2 to 3 hours, occasionally skimming off any excess fat that rises to the top. Strain through a fine strainer into a tall container and leave to cool. If you have time, chill in the refrigerator and lift off any fat that sets on the surface. The stock will keep for 1 to 2 days in the refrigerator, or you can divide it into smaller containers or ice cube trays and freeze until ready to use.

VEGETABLE STOCK

This stock is wonderfully fragrant and is worth making in big batches because it freezes well. You might want to dilute it before using, depending on how long it is left to infuse. Makes about 3¾ cups.

2 tablespoons olive oil   *1 bay leaf*
1 large onion, chopped   *1 star anise*
2 celery sticks, chopped   *1 teaspoon coriander seeds*
1 small fennel bulb, chopped   *½ teaspoon crushed white peppercorns*
2 large carrots, chopped   *1 ounce whole fresh mixed herbs*
1 garlic bulb, sliced in half   *1¼ cups dry white wine*

Heat the oil in a large saucepan. Add the onion and fry until soft but not brown. Stir in the remaining vegetables and bay leaf and cook, stirring, for a minute or so. Pour in 3¾ cups water and bring to a boil. Lower the heat and simmer for 30 minutes.

Add the star anise, coriander seeds, and peppercorns and simmer for 10 minutes. Add the herbs and wine and simmer for 5 minutes longer. Remove from the heat, cover, and leave to infuse in a cold place; the flavor improves for up to 48 hours. Strain through a fine strainer. This will keep in the refrigerator for another 1 to 2 days, or you can divide it into smaller containers or ice cube trays and freeze until ready to use.

FISH STOCK

I have not included salt in this recipe because the stock is greatly reduced so it can become too salty. The seasoning should, therefore, be added when making the soup. Fishmongers often have bones for sale (but not on display) so don't be afraid to ask. Bones from flat fish, such as flounder, are the best to use. Makes about 3¾ cups.

3 pounds fish bones, including heads   *1 bay leaf*
2 celery sticks, chopped   *½ ounce fresh mixed parsley, tarragon,*
2 leeks, chopped   *and chervil stems*
1 large onion, chopped   *6 black peppercorns*
1 large carrot, chopped

Soak the fish bones in cold water for 30 minutes. Drain, rinse well, and roughly chop. Place in a large saucepan with all the remaining ingredients. Cover with about 2 quarts cold water and bring to a boil, skimming off any foam that rises to the surface.

Lower the heat and simmer for 30 minutes without boiling, occasionally skimming the top, if necessary. Remove from the heat and leave to cool completely, which will take 3 to 4 hours.

Strain the stock through a fine strainer into a tall container; if you have time, place in the refrigerator overnight to settle. The next day, skim off any foam that has formed on the top. This will keep for 1 to 2 days in the refrigerator, or you can divide it into smaller containers or ice cube trays, discarding the sediment that will settle at the bottom, and freeze until ready to use.

Rouille

This fiery, hot Provençal sauce is traditionally served with fish soups. It can be served separately in little bowls so it can be used as a dip, spread onto croutons, or just whisked directly into the soup. Makes about ⅔ cup.

1 red bell pepper
1 small slice stale bread
2 garlic cloves, crushed

1 mild red chili, seeded and chopped
Salt and freshly ground black pepper
6 tablespoons extra-virgin olive oil

Heat the broiler. Place the pepper on the broiler rack and broil for 20 to 30 minutes until charred and blistered, turning regularly. Place in a plastic bag, secure with a knot, and leave the pepper to steam in its own heat for 10 minutes. Remove from the bag and peel, seed, and chop the flesh, reserving any juices.

Meanwhile, soak the bread in a little water for about 5 minutes, then squeeze out the excess. Place in a food processor with the pepper flesh, garlic, and chili. Season generously and process to a paste. With the motor running, gradually pour in the oil to make a smooth, shiny sauce. Transfer to a bowl and cover with plastic wrap or store in a screw-top jar. This will keep in the refrigerator for up to 1 week. Return to room temperature before using.

Pestos

These are vibrant, pungent sauces that can be drizzled into soups to garnish or just stirred in at the last moment for extra flavor. I also like to spread them onto croûtes (page 14) or simply use as a dip. Experiment using the suggestions below, then make up your own—the variations are endless.

TRADITIONAL ITALIAN PESTO
Makes about ⅔ cup.

¼ cup pine nuts
½ cup fresh basil leaves
¼ cup freshly grated Parmesan

1 garlic clove, chopped
6 tablespoons extra-virgin olive oil
Sea salt and freshly ground black pepper

Toast the pine nuts in a small, dry skillet until light golden; remove from the heat and leave to cool completely. When cool, place in a food processor with the basil, Parmesan, garlic, and oil. Season generously and process for 30 seconds.

Scrape down the inside of the bowl with a rubber spatula and process again for 30 seconds. Transfer to a bowl and cover with plastic wrap or store in a screw-top jar. This will keep in the refrigerator for up to 1 week; top up with a little olive oil each time you use it to maintain the vibrant color.

VARIATIONS
* Use a combination of basil, flat-leaf parsley, and arugula leaves for a more pronounced, peppery flavor. This is very good with all types of tomato soups.
* Replace the pine nuts with walnuts and use flat-leaf parsley instead of basil for a more robust taste. This combination is good spread on croûtes, topped with sliced goat cheese, and broiled until bubbling; float in the soup to serve.
* Replace the Parmesan with watercress and, instead of the basil, use a combination of chives, tarragon, chervil, and flat-leaf parsley for a sophisticated flavor, which is great with any fish soup.
* Add 2 peeled, seeded, and diced plum tomatoes to the basic mixture. This is excellent with minestrone-style soups.

Salsas

Use only the freshest of ingredients when making salsas and keep them separate until just before you are ready to serve. I like salsas either piled in tiny mounds on tortilla chips, which can then be served with the soup or floating on top, or scattered directly over any chilled summer soup.

SALSA FRESCA
Makes about ⅔ cup.

2 large plum tomatoes, peeled, seeded, and diced
1 small red onion, finely diced
1 garlic clove, minced
1 mild red chili, seeded and minced

Juice of 1 lime
2 tablespoons extra-virgin olive oil
2 tablespoons chopped fresh flat-leaf parsley
Pinch of sugar
Salt and freshly ground black pepper

Place the tomatoes, onion, garlic, chili, lime juice, oil, and parsley in a bowl. Add the sugar and season generously, then stir gently to combine. Serve at room temperature.

VARIATIONS
* For a spicy kick, add ¼ teaspoon each ground coriander and cumin, and replace the parsley with fresh cilantro. Use in robust, bean-based soups.

* For a tropical salsa, replace the tomatoes with 1 large diced mango. This is fantastic with most kinds of Asian soups, especially fish-based ones.

* Replace the tomatoes with corn kernels and the parsley with fresh cilantro. This is perfect to serve with any Mexican-style soup.

* For a milder Mediterranean flavor, omit the red onion and chili and replace the lime juice with a splash of balsamic vinegar and the fresh parsley with basil.

Clockwise from top: Salsa Fresca, Rouille, Traditional Italian Pesto

TO THICKEN SOUP

Plenty of soups don't need thickening; however, some need something to pull all the ingredients and the texture together.

REDUCTION

Soups that don't include cream, yogurt, or eggs can be thickened easily by reduction. Just simmer the soup, uncovered, for 20 to 30 minutes, keeping an eye on the progress until it reaches the required consistency, making sure nothing sticks to the bottom of the pan. Don't forget, however, this process will also intensify the flavors, so put off adding any salt until the end.

OLIVE OIL

One of the best ways to thicken a vegetable soup once it is cooked is to stir in a couple of tablespoons extra-virgin olive oil and return the soup to the boil, then remove it from the heat. You can repeat this process a couple of times with excellent results and, surprisingly, no trace of oiliness.

EGGS AND CREAM

Egg yolks mixed with stock, milk, or cream and added to the soup just before serving will thicken and enrich it beyond belief. Although you need a certain amount of heat to cook the eggs, whatever you do, don't let the soup to boil or they will curdle. Simply add 1 or 2 egg yolks to 4 tablespoons of your chosen liquid for every 2½ cups of soup. Add a ladleful of the hot soup to the egg yolk mixture, stirring until combined, then stir the mixture back into the soup and slowly warm through.

GROUND NUTS

Ground almonds, hazelnuts, and walnuts are traditionally used to thicken soups in Spain and Mexico. Stir about ½ cup into a full quantity of soup and simmer for a few minutes until thickened.

GARNISHES

CROUTONS

Cut the crusts off 4 ounces firm-crumbed bread and cut into ¼-inch cubes, diamonds, or hearts. Heat 4 tablespoons oil or melt 4 tablespoons unsalted butter or other fat in a large skillet. Add the croutons and fry for 5 to 10 minutes, tossing and turning occasionally until golden. For a healthier version, heat the oven to 375°F. Place the croutons in a bowl with 1 tablespoon olive oil and stir gently until coated, then spread out in a single layer on a cookie sheet. Bake for 8 to 10 minutes until crisp and golden. Drain the croutons on paper towels before serving. Croutons can be stored in an airtight container or plastic bag for a few days.

VARIATIONS

* Garlic Croutons: Mix 2 crushed garlic cloves with the oil before tossing it through the bread cubes prior to cooking.

* Parmesan Croutons: Mix 2 tablespoons freshly grated Parmesan with the oil before tossing the bread cubes in it.

* Anchovy Croutons: Mash a drained 2-ounce can of anchovy fillets into the oil until disintegrated, then mix with the bread cubes.

* Olive Croutons: Stir 2 teaspoons black or green olive paste (from a jar) into the oil, then mix with the bread cubes.

* Bacon Croutons: Fry 4 ounces diced pancetta or bacon until crisp, then toss with the finished croutons at the last minute.

CROÛTES

Place thin slices of day-old French bread or ciabatta on a cookie sheet and either bake in an oven heated to its lowest setting or toast under the broiler until dry but not brown. Rub both sides with a peeled garlic clove and drizzle extra-virgin olive oil on top. To make toasted cheese croûtes, top with grated cheese before baking. Alternatively, spread the croûtes with any of the flavor variations above prior to cooking.

PASTRY PUFFS

Heat the oven to 350°F. Stamp or cut out shapes—hearts or stars and moons—from puff pastry dough. Arrange on a waxed-paper-lined cookie sheet and sprinkle with freshly grated Parmesan, poppy seeds, celery seeds, a dusting of paprika, or chopped fresh herbs. Bake for 5 to 10 minutes, depending on the size of the shapes. Cool on a wire rack. Float in bowls of soup to serve.

CHEESE GARNISHES

* Grate cheddar or Gruyère cheese and sprinkle it over each bowl of soup just before serving. Alternatively, swirl in a little extra-virgin olive oil and scatter a few shavings of Parmesan or pecorino on top.

* Cut some quick-melting cheese, such as Gruyère, manchego, fontina, or mozzarella into little cubes and stir into soup just before serving.

CARROT SPAGHETTI
Cut 2 large carrots into neat rectangular blocks and then cut into long, fine strips—a mandoline does this very well. Place in a saucepan and cover with cold water. Add a knob of butter and a pinch of salt, bring to a simmer, and simmer until just tender. Drain and use at once.

CRISPY SEAWEED
Very finely shred leafy greens, such as cabbage, spinach, or kale, and deep-fry in batches at 375°F for 1 to 2 minutes until crispy. Drain on paper towels and season with a little salt and sugar.

VEGETABLE HAIR
This works well with leeks, carrots, parsnips, beets, celeriac, and gingerroot; use them individually or in combination. Peel and cut the vegetables of your choice into julienne strips (use a mandoline if possible) and deep-fry at 375°F for 30 seconds to 1 minute until crisp. Drain on paper towels and season with coarse sea salt.

VEGETABLE CHIPS
Root vegetables, especially parsnips, potatoes, and beets, make fantastic chips. Peel and cut the vegetables into wafer-thin rounds (use a mandoline if possible), rinse, and pat dry. Deep-fry at 375°F for 1 to 2 minutes until crisp and lightly golden. Drain well on paper towels. Pile up on dollops of sour cream.

CRISPY ONIONS
Cut the onions in half lengthwise and thinly slice. Drain between sheets of paper towels for about 30 minutes to draw out moisture. Heat about ½ inch oil in a wok or large skillet and stir-fry the onions for 15 to 20 minutes until deep brown, taking care they don't burn. Sprinkle over spoonfuls of yogurt.

DEEP-FRIED BASIL
This has a wonderful translucent look. Rinse basil leaves and pat dry. Heat 4 tablespoons olive oil until very hot, but not smoking. Remove the pan from the heat and drop in the basil leaves for a few seconds. Remove with a draining spoon and drain on paper towels.

GUACAMOLE
Dice a large, ripe avocado. Combine it with 2 peeled, seeded, and diced tomatoes, a couple tablespoons of chopped fresh cilantro, 4 finely chopped scllions, 1 seeded and diced red chili, and a little crushed garlic. Season to taste.

SALSA VERDE
Place ¼ cup flat-leaf parsley leaves, 12 basil leaves, 6 mint leaves, 1 chopped garlic clove, 1 tablespoon rinsed capers, and 2 chopped anchovy fillets in a mini-blender and process until just blended. Place in a bowl and gradually whisk in 4 tablespoons olive oil and 1 teaspoon each red wine vinegar, lemon juice, and Dijon mustard. Season well.

MINT RELISH
Place ¼ cup fresh mint leaves, 1 seeded and chopped green chili, 2 chopped scallions, ½ teaspoon freshly grated gingerroot, a squeeze of lemon juice, and a good pinch each of salt and sugar in a mini-blender. Add a couple of tablespoons of water and process to a purée.

BASIL PURÉE
This can be made in a mini-blender but I find a mortar and pestle helps to keep the vibrant color for longer. Place ¼ cup fresh basil leaves in a mortar with a good pinch of fine sea salt. Grind for 1 to 2 minutes with a pestle, then work in 2 tablespoons extra-virgin olive oil and 1 teaspoon balsamic vinegar. Season to taste.

BLACK MUSTARD SEED AND ONION TARKA
Heat 4 tablespoons sunflower oil in a skillet. Add 6 tablespoons dried onion flakes and 1 teaspoon black mustard seeds. Stir-fry for 1 minute, then drain well on paper towels. Serve hot or cold, sprinkled over a simple vegetable or lentil soup to give it an extra dimension.

FLAVORED BUTTERS

These are great cut into thin slices and served on top of hot soup. I find they enrich and enhance the existing flavors. They can be made in advance and keep for one week in the refrigerator, or 2 months in the freezer. Each recipe makes about ⅔ cup in total.

TARRAGON BUTTER

⅔ cup dry white wine
2 shallots, minced
½ cup (1 stick) unsalted butter, softened

2 tablespoons chopped fresh tarragon
Fine sea salt and freshly ground
   black pepper

Place the wine and shallots in a small saucepan and boil rapidly until the wine has almost disappeared; leave to cool completely. Gradually beat into the butter with the tarragon. Season to taste. Shape and roll in a piece of waxed paper to make a log. Chill for 2 hours until firm, then use as required.

PIQUANT BUTTER

2 garlic cloves, crushed
1 tablespooon rinsed and minced capers
2 tablespoons chopped fresh flat-leaf parsley

½ cup (1 stick) unsalted butter, softened
Fine sea salt and freshly ground black pepper

Beat the garlic, capers, and flat-leaf parsley into the butter and season to taste. Shape and roll as above.

CHILI AND LIME BUTTER

2 mild red chilies, seeded and minced
Grated zest and juice of 1 small lime
1 tablespoon snipped fresh chives

½ cup (1 stick) unsalted butter
Fine sea salt and freshly ground black pepper

Beat the chilies, lime zest and juice, and chives into the butter and season to taste. Shape and roll as above.

BLUE CHEESE BUTTER

3 ounces blue cheese, such as Roquefort
   or Stilton
1 tablespoon chopped fresh flat-leaf parsley

4 tablespoons unsalted butter, softened
Fine sea salt and freshly ground black pepper

Beat the cheese and flat-leaf parsley into the butter and season to taste. Shape and roll as above.

FLAVORED COOLERS

These are designed to give a contrasting texture, flavor, and temperature to a soup, as well as acting as an attractive garnish. They work well with gutsy, well-flavored, and spicy soups. Just spoon into the middle of the soup; if you like, swirl it out to make a delicate feather pattern, using a toothpick.

SWEET PEPPER CREAM

Broil a red or yellow bell pepper until charred and blistered (see recipe for Rouille on page 12 for full directions), then peel and remove the seeds. Purée the flesh in a mini-blender. Press the purée through a strainer into 4 tablespoons unwhipped heavy cream. Season to taste.

SOUR CREAM COOLER

Mix together ⅔ cup sour cream, 2 peeled, seeded, and diced plum tomatoes, and 2 heaped tablespoons shredded basil. Season generously.

HERB CREAM

Whip ⅔ cup heavy cream until thick but not stiff. Season generously and stir in 3 tablespoons chopped fresh herbs of your choice (if using rosemary or thyme, add only very small amounts, because they have a much stronger, more pronounced flavor than other fresh herbs).

MINT-YOGURT COOLER

Mix together ⅔ cup plain yogurt, 1 crushed garlic clove, and 2 tablespoons chopped fresh mint. Season with a pinch of salt.

LIME-INFUSED YOGURT

This also works well with oranges or lemons. Mix together 1¼ cups Greek-style yogurt or thick plain yogurt wih the finely grated zest and juice of 1 lime; set aside to infuse for 30 minutes. Season generously and add a pinch of freshly grated gingerroot and 2 teaspoons snipped fresh chives.

SAFFRON–MASCARPONE COOLER

I love this with any potato or seafood soup. Soak a good pinch of saffron strands in 1 tablespoon hot water. Beat into 1 cup plus 2 tablespoons mascarpone and season generously.

AIOLI

Have all of the ingredients at room temperature. Place 1 peeled and chopped garlic clove in a mortar and use a pestle to pound to a paste with a pinch of salt, then work in 1 egg yolk. Add ⅔ cup olive oil, drop by drop, until well combined. Stir in 1 tablespoon white-wine vinegar and season well.

Clockwise from top right: Piquant Butter, Tarragon Butter, Chili and Lime Butter, Blue Cheese Butter

HOT & SPICY

These recipes come from all around the world and are for anyone who likes a bit of a kick in their food. "Hotness" is

such a matter of personal taste that I recommend you always use chilies with caution, because they vary greatly in strength.

All recipes serve 4 to 6.

FIERY LENTIL SOUP

The spices give this nutritious soup an excellent flavor. It is similar to a traditional dhal, and makes a good first course for an Indian meal if you reduce it to a slightly thicker purée.

1 tablespoon sunflower oil	3³/4 cups vegetable stock
1 large onion, chopped	Salt and freshly ground black pepper
4 garlic cloves, crushed	4 cups roughly chopped fresh spinach
2 teaspoons ground turmeric	leaves
2 teaspoons garam masala	Juice of 1 lime
1 bay leaf	Plain yogurt and chopped fresh cilantro,
6 cardamom pods, crushed	to garnish
1 heaping cup red or orange lentils, rinsed	

Heat the oil in a large saucepan. Add the onion and fry for 5 to 6 minutes until golden brown. Stir in the garlic, turmeric, garam masala, bay leaf, and cardamom pods and cook slowly for 1 minute until the spices are lightly toasted.

Add the lentils to the saucepan with the stock; season well. Simmer for about 20 minutes, or until the lentils are just tender. Stir in the spinach and cook for 5 minutes longer. Season to taste and add the lime juice. Ladle into bowls and add a spoonful of yogurt and a sprinkling of cilantro. Serve at once.

GARLIC BREAD SOUP

This simple recipe is great to have on hand. I grow all my own herbs on the kitchen windowsill and even have a chili plant that produces all year round.

4 tablespoons olive oil	1 teaspoon paprika
4 ounces Italian pancetta, diced	5 cups chicken or vegetable stock
10 garlic cloves, minced	6 thick slices country bread, crusts removed
2 red chiles, seeded and minced	and cut into cubes
1 heaping teaspoon fresh thyme leaves	Salt and freshly ground black pepper
¹/2 teaspoon chopped fresh sage	

Heat the oil in a large saucepan. Add the pancetta and cook for about 5 minutes until light golden and crispy. Stir in the garlic, chili, thyme, and sage and cook for another few minutes. Stir in the paprika. Pour in the stock, add the bread, and simmer for another 10 minutes, or until the bread breaks down and thickens the soup. Season to taste. Ladle into bowls and serve at once.

CHICKEN, COCONUT, AND GALANGAL SOUP

Coconut milk, one of my favorite ingredients, makes a fantastic, creamy base for all the other robust flavors in this Asian-style soup. It is so simple it literally takes minutes to prepare.

3³/4 cups chicken stock	8 ounces skinless, boneless chicken breast
4 kaffir lime leaves	halves, thinly sliced
2-inch piece galangal, peeled and cut	1³/4 cups coconut milk
into matchsticks	Good pinch dried chili flakes
4 tablespoons Thai fish sauce	4 tablespoons chopped fresh cilantro leaves
Juice of 2 lemons	

Place the stock in a large saucepan with the lime leaves, galangal, fish sauce, and lemon juice. Bring to a boil, stirring continuously. Reduce the heat and simmer for 5 minutes until the galangal is tender. Add the chicken and coconut milk and continue to cook over high heat for 2 minutes, or until the chicken is cooked through and tender. Add the dried chili flakes and cilantro and cook for about 20 seconds longer. Ladle into bowls and serve at once.

JAPANESE MISO SOUP

Instant fish stock (*dashi-no-moto*) and the other ingredients you need for this recipe are readily available in Asian food stores and some supermarkets. There are a number of different types of miso and all make good soup; flavors range from slightly sweet to slightly bitter.

2 tablespoons sunflower oil	1 cup young leaf spinach
3 cups sliced fresh shiitake mushrooms	4 heaping tablespoons miso
5 cups reconstituted Japanese soup stock	Dark soy sauce, to taste
(dashi-no-moto) or light vegetable stock	Lemon peel slivers, to garnish

Heat the oil in a saucepan. Add the mushrooms and sauté for about 5 minutes until tender. Pour in the stock and bring to a boil. Lower the heat, add the spinach, and simmer for a few minutes until the spinach wilts and the mushrooms are tender.

Blend a little of the stock with the miso and stir into the saucepan. Bring almost to a boil and season with soy sauce. Ladle into bowls. Garnish with the lemon peel and serve at once.

Above: Curried Parsnip Soup

CURRIED PARSNIP SOUP

Use a fresh, good-quality curry powder for this soup and not one that has been stuck at the back of the pantry for the last six months.

4 tablespoons unsalted butter
1 onion, minced
1 garlic clove, minced
2 parsnips, chopped
1 potato, diced
2 teaspoons medium-hot curry powder

3³/₄ cups chicken or vegetable stock
Salt and fresh ground black pepper
²/₃ cup heavy cream
Croutons (page 14) and snipped fresh chives, to garnish

Melt the butter in a large saucepan. Add the onion and garlic and cook for 2 to 3 minutes until they begin to soften. Add the parsnips and potato, stir to coat in the butter, cover the pan, and cook 10 minutes, stirring once or twice.

Stir the curry powder into the vegetables and cook for another minute or so, stirring. Pour in the stock and season generously. Bring to a boil. Lower the heat and simmer for 40 minutes, or until the parsnips are tender and the soup has thickened; set aside to cool a little.

Purée the soup in batches in a food processor or with a hand-held blender. To serve, stir in the cream and reheat slowly. Season to taste. Ladle into bowls and garnish with the croutons and chives.

THAI CHICKEN NOODLE SOUP

In Thai cooking, spicy flavors are cut with the acidity of lemons or limes. The secret is in the balance and no one element should dominate.

9 ounces vermicelli rice noodles
2 tablespoons sunflower oil
2 large skinless, boneless chicken breast halves, cut into thin strips
2 garlic cloves, crushed
2 tablespoons Thai red curry paste

5 cups chicken stock
1 head bok choy, thinly sliced
1 bunch scallions, thinly sliced
3 tablespoons light soy sauce
Juice of 1 lemon
Good handful fresh mint leaves

Plunge the noodles into a large saucepan of boiling, salted water. Remove the saucepan from the heat and set aside for 2 minutes, or according to the package directions. Drain and rinse under cold running water; set aside.

Heat the oil in a large saucepan. Add the chicken and cook over high heat for 2 to 3 minutes, stirring until light brown. Stir in the garlic and curry paste and cook for another minute, stirring. Pour in the stock and bring to a boil. Reduce the heat and simmer for 5 minutes, or until the chicken is cooked through and tender.

Stir in the bok choy and scallions and cook for another minute or so until the greens just wilt. Add the soy sauce and lemon juice and remove from the heat. Divide the noodles between serving bowls and scatter the mint leaves over. Ladle in the hot soup. Serve at once.

SWEET POTATO SPLASH

4 tablespoons unsalted butter
1 large onion, minced
1¹/₂ pounds sweet potatoes, peeled and diced
1 teaspoon fresh thyme leaves, plus extra to garnish

Salt and freshly ground black pepper
¹/₂ teaspoon ground allspice
2 red bird's-eye chilies, seeded and minced
3³/₄ cups chicken or vegetable stock
³/₄ cup crème fraîche or sour cream

Melt the butter in a large, heavy-bottomed saucepan with a tight-fitting lid. Add the onion and cook for 2 to 3 minutes until just beginning to soften. Stir in the sweet potatoes until well coated. Add the thyme and season generously. Place a parchment-paper circle directly on top to keep in the steam. Cover the saucepan and sweat over low heat for about 10 minutes until the sweet potatoes are soft but not colored.

Remove the lid and the paper, stir in the allspice and chilies, and cook for another minute, stirring. Pour in the stock and bring to a boil. Lower the heat and simmer for 10 minutes, or until the sweet potatoes are tender. Purée the soup in batches in a food processor or with a hand-held blender. Pour back into the pan and season to taste. Stir in two-thirds of the crème fraîche or sour cream and reheat slowly. Ladle into bowls and add spoonfuls of the remaining crème fraîche or sour cream. Garnish with thyme leaves and serve at once.

THAI MIXED FISH SOUP

This is the basic method for making Thai *tom yam* soup so you can experiment with your choice of fish and shellfish. Try it with a mixture of scallops, mussels, squid, and crab claws.

5 cups chicken or vegetable stock
1-inch piece galangal, peeled and chopped
2 lemongrass stalks, lightly crushed and chopped
3 kaffir lime leaves, minced
1 tablespoon grilled chili oil (tom yam sauce)
2 red bird's-eye chilies, seeded and minced
Juice of 1 lemon

4 tablespoons Thai fish sauce
½ teaspoon sugar
12 ounces firm white fish fillets, skinned and cut into chunks
4 ounces raw jumbo shrimp, shelled and deveined
4 scallions, minced
2 tablespoons roughly chopped fresh cilantro

Place the stock in a saucepan with the galangal, lemongrass, lime leaves, and chili oil and bring to a boil. Lower the heat and simmer for 15 minutes; strain into a clean saucepan.

Add the chilies, lemon juice, fish sauce, and sugar to the flavored stock and simmer for 2 minutes, Add the fish, shrimp, and scallions and simmer 2 to 3 minutes longer until all the seafood is just tender. Ladle into soup bowls and sprinkle the cilantro over to serve.

CHINESE SHRIMP-BALL SOUP

This refreshing soup is made glamorous by the addition of the shrimp balls. Although they are expensive to make using the raw jumbo shrimp or tiger prawns, the flavor makes it well worth it.

Peanut oil for deep-frying
1 pound raw jumbo shrimp or tiger prawns, shelled and deveined
1 ounce pork fat
1 egg white
2 scallions, minced
1 green chili, seeded and minced
1 teaspoon freshly grated gingerroot

Salt and freshly ground black pepper
1½ quarts chicken stock
3 tablespoons rice wine or dry sherry
2 tablespoons light soy sauce
1 teaspoon sugar
2 teaspoons sesame oil
8 ounces fresh watercress, large stems removed

Heat 2 inches oil in a skillet to 375°F. Meanwhile, place the shrimp, pork fat, egg white, scallions, chili, and ginger in a food processor. Add 1 teaspoon salt and ¼ teaspoon pepper and process briefly to make a smooth paste. Form spoonfuls of the paste into balls, about 1 inch in diameter. Carefully drop the balls into the hot oil and deep-fry for 3 to 4 minutes until puffed up and golden brown. Drain well on paper towels.

Place the stock in a large saucepan with the wine or sherry, soy sauce, and sugar. Bring to a simmer and simmer for 3 minutes. Add the shrimp balls and cook for 2 minutes. Stir in the sesame oil, season to taste, and remove from the heat. Divide the watercress between the serving bowls, ladle the soup and shrimp balls over, and serve at once.

ASIAN CHICKEN AND CORN SOUP

This is a variation on an old favorite that has stood the test of time. It appears in some form on almost every Chinese takeout menu, but I really like the fresh flavors of this version.

2 tablespoons sunflower oil
2 garlic cloves, minced
1-inch piece fresh gingeroot, peeled and minced
2 green bird's-eye chilies, seeded and minced
2 skinless, boneless chicken breast halves, finely sliced
2 tablespoons cornstarch

5 cups chicken stock
1½ cups corn kernels, thawed if frozen
2 eggs
Juice of 1 lemon
Salt and freshly ground black pepper
About 2 teaspoons dark soy sauce
2 tablespoons roughly chopped fresh cilantro leaves

Heat the oil in a large saucepan. Add the garlic, ginger, and chilies and stir-fry for 30 seconds or so. Add the chicken and stir-fry for 3 to 4 minutes until well sealed. Blend the cornstarch with a little of the stock and add to the pan with the remaining stock and the corn. Bring to a boil, stirring continuously. Lower the heat and simmer for about 5 minutes.

Beat together the eggs and lemon juice. Slowly trickle the mixture into the soup, stirring with a chopstick or fork to make egg strands. Season to taste and pour into serving bowls. Add a drizzle of soy sauce and scatter the cilantro over. Serve at once.

Above: Thai Mixed Fish Soup

MOROCCAN BEAN SOUP

It really makes a huge difference in flavor if you grind your own spices. If you haven't got a mini-blender, a mortar and pestle works just as well—it just takes a bit more time.

½ small cinnamon stick	5 cups chicken or vegetable stock
2 whole cloves	1 pound new potatoes, quartered
½ teaspoon each yellow mustard, cumin, and coriander seeds	1 can (14-oz.) garbanzo beans, drained and rinsed
2 tablespoons olive oil	Salt and freshly ground black pepper
1 onion, chopped	⅔ cup shredded spinach leaves
1 red bell pepper, seeded and cut into strips	Harissa (hot chili sauce), to taste

Warm a small skillet over the stove. Add the cinnamon stick and cloves with the mustard, cumin, and coriander seeds. Toast for a couple of minutes until they start to smell aromatic, tossing occasionally. Place the spices in a mini-blender and grind to a powder.

Heat the oil in a large saucepan. Add the onion and pepper and cook for 2 to 3 minutes until the onion is soft but not brown. Sprinkle in the spice mixture and cook for another minute or so, stirring. Pour in the stock and add the potatoes and beans. Season to taste. Bring to a simmer and simmer for 15 minutes, or until the potatoes are tender.

Stir in the spinach and the harissa to taste (I recommend about 2 tablespoons) and cook until the spinach just wilts. Ladle into bowls, piling up some of the chunky ingredients in the middle of each bowl to serve.

SPICY EGGPLANT AND TOMATO SOUP

This delicious soup has lots of Asian undertones. I like to serve it with mint yogurt as it tempers the flavors, providing a great contrast.

6 tablespoons olive oil	1 teaspoon ground coriander
3 cups sliced eggplant, cut into ¾-inch slices	1 teaspoon fennel seeds
1 large onion, minced	Salt and freshly ground black pepper
2 garlic cloves, minced	1 can (14-oz.) crushed tomatoes
1 red Scotch bonnet chili, seeded and minced	3¾ cups vegetable stock
	1¾ cups coconut milk
1 teaspoon ground cumin	Mint-yogurt cooler (page 16), to garnish

Heat 4 tablespoons of the oil in a large skillet. Add the eggplant slices and cook in batches until lightly golden. Drain on paper towels, then roughly chop; set aside.
Heat the remaining oil in a large saucepan. Add the onion and slowly fry for about 10 minutes until lightly caramelized. Add the garlic, chili, and spices and cook for 2 minutes longer. Season generously.
Add the reserved eggplant, the tomatoes, stock, and coconut milk. Bring to a boil, lower the heat, and simmer for 20 minutes until slightly reduced and thicker. Season to taste.
Leave to cool a little, then purée in batches in a food processor or with a hand-held blender until smooth. Return to a clean saucepan and reheat slowly. Season to taste and ladle into bowls. Add a good spoonful of the mint-yogurt cooler and serve at once.

CHINESE MUSHROOM SOUP

Dried Chinese mushrooms are sold in most oriental grocery stores. Look out for shiitake and wood-ears; I like a combination of both in this soup.

1 ounce dried Chinese mushrooms (see headnote)	2 tablespoons sunflower oil
½-ounce bunch fresh cilantro	5 cups vegetable or chicken stock
1-inch piece gingerroot, peeled and chopped	2 tablespoons Thai fish sauce
2 garlic cloves, chopped	2 ounces vermicelli rice noodles
4 scallions, sliced on the diagonal, with white and green parts separated	1 head of bok choy, shredded
	Juice of 1 lime
	Good pinch of sugar

Place the mushrooms in a bowl and cover with hot water; set aside to soak and swell for 10 minutes. Drain, reserving ⅔ cup of the soaking liquid. Trim off the tough stems and cut the caps into slices. Set aside. Chop the cilantro, reserving some leaves for garnish. Place the cilantro in a mini-blender with the ginger, garlic, and the white parts of the scallions. Process to a paste.

Heat the oil in a large saucepan. Add the cilantro paste and stir-fry for 1 minute. Pour in the stock and add the reserved soaking liquid with the mushrooms and fish sauce. Bring to a boil and skim any foam off the surface. Lower the heat and simmer for 15 minutes until the mushrooms are tender.

Place the noodles in a saucepan of boiling water, remove from the heat, and leave to soak for 4 minutes, or according to the package directions. Drain and rinse with cold water. Add the noodles to the soup with the bok choy, lime juice, and sugar and heat until the bok choy just wilts. Spoon into bowls and garnish with the green scallions and cilantro leaves.

Right: Moroccan Bean Soup

Roasted Tomato and Chili Soup

You can pass this soup through a strainer for a smooth texture, but I don't normally bother. If you are not going to strain the soup, however, cut the eyes out of the tomatoes when you halve them, because they are tough and won't break down during cooking.

1½ pounds plum tomatoes, halved
Sea salt and freshly ground black pepper
2 mild red chilies, halved and seeded
1 large garlic clove, halved
12 large basil leaves
4 tablespoons extra-virgin olive oil, plus extra to garnish

3¾ cups chicken or vegetable stock
10 ounces olive oil-based bread, such as ciabatta, crusts removed
Pared Parmesan shavings, to garnish

Preheat the oven to 400°F. Put the tomatoes in a roasting pan, cut sides up, and season generously. Add the chilies, garlic, and 6 of the basil leaves. Drizzle half of the oil over the top. Roast for 20 to 25 minutes until the tomatoes are soft and lightly charred around the edges.

Tip the tomato mixture into a food processor and process until just blended. Pass through a strainer, if desired, and place in a large saucepan. Pour in the stock and season to taste. Simmer for 5 minutes until well mixed and thick.

Break the bread into small chunks and stir into the soup until the bread is soft and is mixed with the tomatoes. Tear the remaining basil leaves into small pieces and stir into the soup. Ladle into bowls and garnish with Parmesan shavings and a drizzle of oil. Serve at once.

Mulligatawny Soup

Here's a simple version of a classic curried soup. You can also omit the cream and leave the soup chunky for a more substantial meal.

4 tablespoons unsalted butter
1 large onion, minced
1 heaping tablespoon good-quality medium curry paste
2 carrots, diced
1 parsnip, diced
1 potato, diced

1½ cups diced cremini mushrooms
3¾ cups vegetable stock
⅔ cup heavy cream
2 tablespoons chopped fresh cilantro leaves
Juice of ½ lemon
Salt and freshly ground black pepper
1 apple, peeled, cored, and diced

Melt the butter in a large saucepan. Add most of the onion, reserving a little for a garnish, and cook slowly for about 10 minutes until lightly caramelized. Stir in the curry paste and cook for another minute or so, stirring. Add the vegetables and cook for 2 to 3 minutes longer. Pour in the stock and bring to a boil. Lower the heat and simmer for 30 minutes, or until the vegetables are tender. Leave to cool a little.

Purée in batches in a food processor or with a hand-held blender until smooth. Return to a clean saucepan, adding a little water if the soup needs thinning down. Add the cream and cilantro and reheat slowly. Add a little of the lemon juice and season to taste. Ladle into bowls. Mix the reserved onion with the apple and the remaining lemon juice and sprinkle over the soup to serve.

Hot-and-Sour Shrimp Soup

This spicy oriental soup will certainly revive your senses at the end of the day. How hot you make it is up to you—bird's-eye chillies are very fiery, so reduce the quantity if you are unsure.

1 tablespoon chili oil
1 pound raw jumbo shrimp, shelled and deveined, with shells reserved
3¾ cups chicken stock
2 lemongrass stalks, roughly chopped
4 kaffir lime leaves
3 red bird's-eye chilies, minced

1 star anise
Juice of 2 lemons
6 tablespoons Thai fish sauce
1 teaspoon sugar
8 ounces canned straw mushrooms, drained and rinsed
Fresh cilantro leaves, to garnish

Heat the oil in a large saucepan. Add the shrimp shells and sauté until the shells turn bright pink. Pour in the stock, add the lemongrass, lime leaves, chilies, and star anise and bring to a boil. Lower the heat and simmer for 15 minutes to allow the flavors to infuse. Strain through a fine strainer into a clean pan.

Add the lemon juice, fish sauce, and sugar and simmer for 2 minutes longer. Add the shrimp and mushrooms, stir, and cook for 2 to 3 minutes longer until the shrimp are cooked through. Ladle into soup bowls and serve at once.

Turkey-Wonton Laksa

In Malaysia, *laksa* is the name of a creamy coconut, rice, and noodle dish. This variation was made up to use the leftover Christmas turkey.

1 tablespoon sunflower oil
2 heaping teaspoons freshly grated gingerroot
2 garlic cloves, minced
1 teaspoon ground turmeric
1 teaspoon ground coriander
2 heaping tablespoons Thai red curry paste
2½ cups chicken stock
1¾ cups coconut milk

1 heaping cup finely chopped cooked turkey
Good dash light soy sauce
1 teaspoon sesame oil
4 tablespoons roughly chopped fresh cilantro
18 wonton skins
6 ounces rice vermicelli noodles
Juice of 1 lime
4 scallions, thinly sliced

Heat the oil in a large saucepan. Add half of the ginger and garlic, the turmeric, ground coriander, and curry paste and cook for a minute or so, stirring. Pour in the stock and coconut milk and bring to a boil. Lower the heat and simmer for 8 to 10 minutes.

Place the turkey in a bowl with the remaining ginger and garlic, the soy sauce, and sesame oil. Add half of the fresh cilantro and stir to mix. Place 1 heaping teaspoon into each wonton skin, brush the edges with a little water, and bring them up to form a triangular bundle, pressing the edges together to seal. Arrange the wontons in a steamer set over the pan of soup and steam for 4 to 5 minutes until transparent.

Place the noodles in a pan of boiling water and remove from the heat; set aside for 3 to 4 minutes, or according to the package directions. Drain and place some in each serving bowl. Stir the lime juice into the soup. Ladle over the noodles and arrange the wontons on top. Scatter the remaining cilantro and scallions over to serve.

Right: Roasted Tomato and Chili Soup

ENTERTAINING

Entertaining, whatever the occasion, can take hours of preparation, yet the results can be devoured by your guests in a matter of minutes. The great thing about the soups in this chapter is that you can make all of them in advance and keep them chilled in the refrigerator (and most can be frozen), ready for every occasion. All recipes serve 4 to 6.

CRAB BISQUE

This is an extremely rich soup so serve it in small amounts if you want your guests to have any room left for other courses! You can substitute lobster for the crab for an even more decadent flavor.

1¹/2 pounds cooked crabmeat,
    still in the shell
¹/2 cup (1 stick) unsalted butter
About 1 cup each diced onion, carrot, leek,
    celery, and fennel
1 fresh bouquet garni
4 ripe tomatoes, quartered

4 tablespoons brandy (Cognac if possible)
2 teaspoons tomato paste
²/3 cup dry white wine
3³/4 cups fish stock
Salt and freshly ground black pepper
Tarragon herb cream, to serve (page 16)

Remove the white and brown crabmeat from the legs, back shell, and body, discarding the dead man's fingers. Place pieces of the shell in a plastic bag and smash into small pieces.

Melt half the butter in a large saucepan. Add the diced vegetables, stirring to coat them in the butter. Add the crushed crab shell and bouquet garni, stir well, cover, and cook for 10 to 15 minutes until the vegetables are soft but not colored.

Add the tomatoes to the saucepan and cook for 5 minutes longer. Increase the heat and pour in the brandy; it should boil down and reduce immediately. Add the tomato paste, wine, and stock and bring to a simmer, then continue to simmer for 30 minutes until well flavored and slightly reduced. Season to taste.

Press the crab-shell mixture through a fine strainer, pressing out as much liquid as possible with the back of a ladle or a wooden spoon. Ladle the strained liquid into a food processor and add the remaining butter and the most of the crabmeat, reserving some of the white meat to garnish. Process until blended.

Return the soup to a clean saucepan and season to taste. Reheat slowly, then ladle into bowls. Add a sprinkling of the reserved crabmeat and a spoonful of the tarragon herb cream to serve.

BOUILLABAISSE

This soup is renowned the world over and for a very good reason. It uses a whole selection of Mediterranean fish and shellfish to produce a very intense, saffron-flavored broth, which is served separately from the fish and potatoes.

2 pounds prepared mixed fish and
    shellfish, such as small pieces of
    bass, porgy, or monkfish fillets,
    and clams, mussels, and whole
    shrimp
2 large onions, halved and thinly sliced
2 large garlic cloves, crushed
1 celery stick, diced
12 ounces waxy potatoes, thickly
    sliced and rinsed
1¹/2 cups peeled and chopped tomatoes
Thinly shredded peel of ¹/2 orange

1 bay leaf
1 sprig each fresh thyme and fennel
2 whole cloves
2 to 5 black peppercorns
³/4 cup olive oil
Sea salt
1¹/2 quarts boiling water
Few saffron strands soaked in 1 tablespoon
    hot water
Rouille and Croûtes (pages 12 and 14),
    to garnish

Discard any cracked or open clams or mussels that do not close when tapped. Place the onions, garlic, celery, potatoes, and tomatoes in a large saucepan with the orange peel, herbs, and spices. Pour half of the olive oil over and season generously with salt. Pour in the boiling water and bring to a boil. Lower the heat, cover, and simmer for 10 minutes.

Arrange the fish on top and pour the remaining oil and the saffron over. Return to a boil and cover. Lower the heat and simmer for 8 minutes longer. Add the shellfish, cover again, and continue to simmer for another 5 minutes, or until the shellfish have just opened and the fish are still holding their shape. Discard any unopened mussels and clams.

Carefully remove the fish and shellfish from the pan and arrange on a large platter with the potatoes. Ladle the broth into bowls and serve both at the same time with the rouille and croûtes in separate bowls.

SAFFRON–MUSSEL SOUP

This has to be one of the finest dishes I have ever eaten. Don't overcook the leeks or they will lose their vibrant green color.

4¹/₂ pounds fresh mussels, cleaned
1¹/₄ cups dry white wine
1 teaspoon medium curry powder
1 teaspoon sugar
2 garlic cloves, peeled
Good pinch saffron strands, soaked in 1 tablespoon hot water

2 tablespoons unsalted butter
2 large shallots, minced
2 leeks, sliced
3 cups fish stock
²/₃ cup heavy cream
2 tablespoons snipped fresh chives
Salt and freshly ground black pepper

Discard any cracked or open mussels that do not close when tapped. Place the wine, curry powder, sugar, and garlic in a large saucepan and season with pepper. Bring to a boil. Stir in the saffron and add the mussels. Cover and cook over high heat for 3 to 5 minutes, shaking the pan occasionally, until all the mussels open. Drain, reserving the cooking liquid in a bowl and discarding the garlic and any mussels that have not opened. When the mussels are cool enough to handle, remove most of them from their shells, reserving a few whole ones for garnish.

Melt the butter in the saucepan. Add the shallots and cook for about 5 minutes until soft but not brown, stirring occasionally. Add the leeks and cook for another few minutes until soft but still holding their color. Pour in the stock and strain in the reserved mussel cooking liquid through a piece of double cheesecloth to remove any sand and grit. Bring to a simmer and add the mussels, cream, and chives to heat through, without boiling. Season to taste. Ladle into bowls and garnish with the reserved whole mussels to serve.

WILD MUSHROOM SOUP

Soup made from wild mushrooms has the most extraordinary, intense flavor. I find they make the best soup when they are a few days old and have darkened a little.

1 ounce dried cèpe mushrooms
²/₃ cup boiling water
4 tablespoons unsalted butter
1 onion, minced
1 garlic clove, crushed
6 cups sliced wild mushrooms

2¹/₂ cups chicken stock
2 slices white bread, crusts removed
Salt and freshly ground black pepper
²/₃ cup light cream
Parmesan croutons (page 14), to garnish

Soak the dried cèpes in the boiling water for 15 minutes. Drain, reserving the soaking liquid. Finely chop the cèpes; set aside.

Melt the butter in a large saucepan. Add the onion and garlic and cook for 10 minutes until soft but not colored. Increase the heat, add the fresh mushrooms, and stir-fry for 3 to 4 minutes until just tender. Pour in the chicken stock and reserved mushroom soaking liquid; add the reconstituted cèpes and bring to a boil. Lower the heat and simmer for 15 to 20 minutes until the mushrooms are tender and the liquid slightly reduced.

Tear pieces of the bread into the soup and season to taste. Purée in batches in a food processor or with a hand-held blender. Pour back into the clean saucepan, season to taste, and add the cream. Reheat slowly; do not boil. Ladle into bowls and garnish with Parmesan croutons. Serve at once.

ARTICHOKE AND BACON SOUP

When you prepare the artichokes, place them immediately in a bowl of water with a good squeeze of lemon juice to stop them turning brown. You can fry extra bacon and reserve to use as a garnish with swirls of unwhipped cream, instead of the blue cheese butter, if you like.

2 tablespoons sunflower oil
4 ounces ¹/₂-inch-thick slices of slab bacon
2 tablespoons unsalted butter
1 large onion, minced
5 cups peeled and thinly sliced Jerusalem artichokes

3³/₄ cups vegetable stock
Salt and freshly ground black pepper
Thin slices of blue cheese butter (page 16), to garnish

Heat the oil in a large saucepan. Add the bacon and cook for about 5 minutes, stirring occasionally, until crisp. Add the butter and then add the onion, stirring to coat. Lower the heat and cook very slowly for 8 to 10 minutes until the onion is soft but not brown.

Drain the artichokes (see headnote) and add to the saucepan with the stock. Season to taste and bring to a boil. Lower the heat and simmer for about 30 minutes until the artichokes are tender.

Purée the soup in batches in a food processor or with a hand-held blender. Pour into a clean saucepan, season to taste, and reheat slowly. Ladle into bowls and garnish with thin slices of the blue cheese butter.

Right: Saffron–Mussel Soup

WATERCRESS AND POTATO SOUP

You can also serve this chilled, garnished with crumbled Roquefort cheese for a special treat. Roasting the garlic gives the soup an underlying smoky taste, which is sublime.

4 large garlic cloves, unpeeled
2 tablespoons olive oil
2 tablespoons unsalted butter
1 onion, minced
2 bunches fresh watercress
1½ cups diced potatoes
3¾ cups chicken or vegetable stock
Salt and freshly ground black pepper
2 egg yolks

Preheat the oven to 400°F. Place the garlic in a very small roasting pan and drizzle half of the oil over the top. Roast for 25 to 30 minutes until very tender and lightly charred. Leave until cool enough to handle, then slip the flesh out of the skins; reserve.

Heat the remaining oil with the butter in a saucepan. Add the onion and fry for 2 to 3 minutes until soft but not brown. Chop up the watercress, separating the leaves and stems. Add the watercress stems to the onion with the potatoes, cover, and cook slowly for 10 minutes until the potatoes are almost tender but not brown, stirring occasionally.

Pour in the stock, season to taste, and bring to a boil. Lower the heat and simmer for 20 minutes until the potatoes are completely soft and the soup has thickened slightly. Add the roasted garlic with the reserved watercress leaves, putting some aside for garnish, and simmer for 1 minute. Remove from the heat and leave to cool a little.

Purée in batches in a food processor or with a hand-held blender. Pour back into a clean saucepan, season to taste, and reheat slowly. Beat together the egg yolks and cream and stir a ladleful of the soup into the mixture. Stir the mixture into the soup and just warm through; do not boil. Ladle into bowls and garnish with the reserved watercress leaves to serve.

ROYAL SALMON SOUP

I love all fish soups, but this one has a wonderful rich flavor that is hard to beat, especially when it is served with garlic croûtes spread with rouille. For a smoother, more velvety finish, pass the soup through a fine strainer.

3 tablespoons unsalted butter
1 large onion, chopped
2 carrots, chopped
2 celery sticks, chopped
1 small fennel bulb, chopped
4 plum tomatoes, peeled, seeded,
  and chopped
2 heaping tablespoons each chopped fresh
  basil and tarragon
Pinch of saffron strands, soaked in 1 tablespoon
  hot water
1¼ cups dry white wine
3¾ cups fish stock
1 teaspoon tomato paste
10 ounces salmon fillets,
  skinned and chopped
Salt and freshly ground black pepper
Garlic croûtes with rouille
  (pages 14 and 12)

Melt the butter in a large saucepan. Add the onion, carrots, celery, fennel, and tomatoes and cook slowly for about 5 minutes, stirring, until almost tender but not colored. Stir in the herbs and saffron and cook for another 1 to 2 minutes. Pour in the white wine and let reduce a little. Add the fish stock and tomato paste and simmer for 10 to 15 minutes until all the flavors blend and the vegetables are tender.

Stir the salmon into the soup and simmer for another 5 minutes or so until the salmon is just tender and cooked through. Season to taste. Purée the soup in batches in a food processor or with a hand-held blender and push through a fine strainer, if desired. Pour back into a clean saucepan, season to taste, and reheat slowly. Ladle into bowls and serve at once with the rouille-topped croûtes.

Right: Watercress and Potato Soup

TOMATO SOUP WITH FISH QUENELLES

Because the fish quenelles are made from a mousselike mixture, it is very important to keep the mixture as cold as possible at all times so you achieve a light and fluffy result.

1/2 pound sole or flounder fillets,
   skinned, chopped, and chilled
1 egg white, chilled
Grated zest of 1 lemon
1 tablespoon snipped fresh chives
Salt and freshly ground black pepper
1/2 cup heavy cream, chilled
2 tablespoons olive oil

1 onion, minced
2 garlic cloves, minced
1 small fennel bulb, minced, with fronds
   reserved
2 cups peeled and chopped ripe tomatoes
2/3 cup dry white wine
3 3/4 cups fish stock

To make the quenelles, place the fish in a food processor and process until finely ground. With the motor running, slowly pour in the egg white and blend until just combined. Transfer to a bowl, cover with plastic wrap, and chill for 30 minutes. Stir in the lemon zest and chives and season to taste. Gradually beat in the cream, a little at a time, until combined. Cover with plastic wrap and chill for 30 minutes longer.

Heat the oil in a large saucepan. Add the onion and garlic and cook for 5 minutes until soft. Add the fennel and cook for 5 minutes, stirring occasionally. Add the tomatoes and wine and continue to cook for 10 minutes until reduced and thicker. Pour in the stock, season to taste, and bring to a boil. Lower the heat and simmer for 15 minutes until the fennel is tender and the soup is slightly thicker; set aside to cool a little.

Purée the soup in batches in a food processor or with a hand-held blender. Season and pass through a strainer back into a clean saucepan.

To make the quenelles, shape the fish mixture into 12 to 18 quenelle shapes with 2 dessert spoons and place straight into a saucepan of simmering, salted water. Cook for 1 minute, or until they rise to the top. Drain on paper towels.

Reheat the soup and ladle into bowls. Arrange 3 quenelles in each bowl and garnish with the fennel fronds. Serve at once.

VICHYSSOISE

This classic soup was invented by a Frenchman living in the United States. It is always served chilled and has provided the inspiration for many, many variations by world-famous chefs.

4 tablespoons unsalted butter
1 1/2 cups finely chopped small leeks
1 onion, minced
1 1/2 cups diced potatoes
1 celery stick, diced
1 garlic clove, crushed

Salt and freshly ground pepper
3 3/4 cups chicken stock
2/3 cup milk
2/3 cup heavy cream
Snipped fresh chives, to garnish

Melt the butter in a large, heavy-bottomed saucepan. As soon as it foams, stir in the leeks, onion, potatoes, and celery until well coated. Add the garlic and season generously. Press a circle of buttered parchment paper on top of the vegetables. Cover the saucepan with a tight-fitting lid and cook over low heat for about 10 minutes, shaking the pan occasionally, until the vegetables are soft but just beginning to color.

Remove the lid and the paper from the saucepan, pour in the stock, and bring to a boil. Lower the heat and simmer for about 5 minutes until the potatoes are tender. Purée the soup in batches in a food processor or with a hand-held blender.

Push the puréed soup through a fine strainer into a large bowl. Season to taste and stir in the milk and most of the cream, reserving some for garnish. Cover with plastic wrap and chill for at least 2 hours; overnight is best. To serve, ladle into bowls and swirl in the reserved cream. Garnish with the chives and serve chilled.

CHILLED MELON SOUP

What could be more refreshing than a bowl of icy melon soup on a hot summer's day? For an attractive presentation, use 6 small melons instead of 3. Cut a 1-inch slice off the top of each one and hollow them out so you can serve the soup inside the shells. Prop the lids alongside.

3 ripe cantaloupes
6 scallions, minced
4 tablespoons elderflower cordial (optional)
1 heaping tablespoon chopped fresh dill,
   plus extra sprigs, to garnish

3/4 cup plus 2 tablespoons crème fraîche
   or sour cream
About 2 cups non-carbonated mineral water
Salt and freshly ground black pepper
Lime-infused yogurt (page 16), to garnish

Cut each melon in half and discard the seeds, then scoop out the flesh and roughly chop, reserving the juices. Place the melon flesh in a food processor with the scallions, elderflower cordial, if using, dill, and crème fraîche or sour cream. Process to a purée and transfer to a bowl. Stir in any reserved juice and enough of the water to give the required consistency. Season to taste.

Cover the soup with plastic wrap and chill for at least 2 hours; overnight is best. To serve, stir the soup and ladle into bowls. Add spoonfuls of the lime-infused yogurt and garnish with dill sprigs.

Right: Tomato Soup with Fish Quenelles

SHRIMP AND FENNEL SOUP

This soup has a surprisingly delicate flavor with subtle aniseed tones. If you buy whole shrimp, peel them and then bash the shells with a rolling pin. Place the shells in a pan with the fish stock and simmer for about 20 minutes. Strain before using for a much more intensely flavored stock.

4 tablespoons unsalted butter
2 large fennel bulbs, minced, with fronds reserved
4 large shallots, minced
4 tablespoons Pernod
2/3 cup dry white wine
Salt and freshly ground black pepper
3 3/4 cups fish stock
1 pound shelled raw shrimp, deveined
2/3 cup heavy cream

Melt the butter in a large saucepan. Add the fennel and shallots and cook slowly for 20 to 30 minutes, stirring occasionally, until the vegetables are soft and beginning to caramelize. Add the Pernod and let it bubble away completely, stirring constantly. Pour in the wine and simmer for about 5 minutes until reduced by half. Season to taste.

Pour in the stock and bring to a boil. Lower the heat and simmer for 15 to 20 minutes until the flavors are blended and the soup has reduced slightly. Purée the soup in batches in a food processor or with a hand-held blender.

Push the puréed soup through a fine strainer back into a clean saucepan and stir in the shrimp and cream. Season to taste and reheat slowly for 2 to 3 minutes until the shrimp turn pink and opaque; do not boil. Ladle into bowls. Add a good grinding of black pepper and sprinkle the reserved fennel fronds on top. Serve at once.

SWEET POTATO AND COCONUT SOUP

This soup has both Thai and Caribbean influences, and tastes out of this world. It is one of my all-time favorites.

4 tablespoons unsalted butter
4 large shallots, minced
3 cups peeled and diced sweet potatoes
2 red bird's-eye chilies, seeded and minced
1/2-ounce bunch fresh cilantro, stems and leaves minced separately
1 1/2 cups peeled, seeded, and diced plum tomatoes
3 3/4 cups chicken stock
1 3/4 cups coconut milk
Salt and freshly ground black pepper
Crispy seaweed (page 15), to garnish

Melt the butter in a large, heavy-bottomed saucepan. Add the shallots and cook for 2 to 3 minutes until just beginning to soften. Stir in the sweet potatoes until coated. Press a circle of buttered parchment paper on top of the vegetables. Cover the pan with a tight-fitting lid and cook slowly over low heat for about 10 minutes, shaking the pan occasionally, until the sweet potatoes are soft but not colored.

Remove the lid and the paper and stir in the chilies, cilantro stems, and tomatoes. Cook for 1 to 2 minutes, stirring. Pour in the stock and coconut milk and bring to a boil. Lower the heat and simmer for 20 to 25 minutes until the sweet potatoes are tender and the liquid has slightly reduced.

Stir the cilantro leaves into the soup and then purée in batches in a food processor or with a hand-held blender. Pour back into the saucepan, season to taste, and reheat slowly. Ladle into bowls and top with small mounds of crispy seaweed; serve at once.

ASPARAGUS AND MASCARPONE TORTE SOUP

If you can't find imported mascarpone torte cheese, use three ounces each mascarpone and gorgonzola cheeses.

1½ pounds asparagus, woody ends
  removed
4 tablespoons unsalted butter
2 large shallots, minced
1 potato, diced

3¾ cups chicken or vegetable stock
Salt and freshly ground black pepper
6 ounces mascarpone torte cheese, crumbled
4 tablespoons light cream

Cut the top 2 inches off the asparagus spears. Cook them slowly in boiling water for 3 to 4 minutes until just tender. Drain well and refresh under cold water; set aside. Slice the stalks.

Melt the butter in a large saucepan. Add the shallots, potato, and asparagus, cover, and cook slowly for 10 minutes until soft but not colored, stirring once or twice. Pour in the stock, season to taste, and bring to a boil. Lower the heat and simmer for 20 minutes until the potatoes are tender and the soup has thickened slightly.

Purée the soup in batches in a food processor or with a hand-held blender. Return to the saucepan and whisk in most of the cheese, reserving some for a garnish. Season to taste and reheat slowly; do not boil. Serve hot or chilled. Ladle into bowls, top with a swirl of the cream and garnish with the reserved asparagus tips and crumbled mascarpone torte.

CREAM OF CELERIAC SOUP

Celeriac is an unusual looking root vegetable with a subtle, celerylike flavor. Choose your specimen carefully: If you buy a particularly knobby one, you'll waste a lot of it when you peel it.

4 tablespoons unsalted butter
1½ pounds celeriac, peeled and
  diced
1 large onion, minced
3¾ cups vegetable stock

4 tablespoons light cream
Squeeze of lemon juice
Salt and freshly ground black pepper
Dill herb cream (page 16), to garnish

Melt the butter in a large saucepan. Add the celeriac and onion and cook slowly for 1 to 2 minutes, stirring constantly. Press a buttered circle of parchment paper onto the vegetables and cover with a tight-fitting lid. Cook slowly for about 10 minutes, shaking the pan occasionally, until the vegetables are soft and have just started to color.

Remove the lid and paper. Pour in the stock and bring to a boil. Lower the heat and simmer for 25 to 30 minutes until the celeriac is tender and the liquid has reduced slightly. Purée in batches in a food processor or with a hand-held blender.

Push the puréed soup through a fine strainer into a clean saucepan and stir in the cream and lemon juice. Season to taste and reheat slowly until just warmed through; do not boil. Ladle into bowls and add a good spoonful of the dill herb cream. Serve at once.

Above: *Asparagus and Mascarpone Torte Soup*

WHITE GARLIC GAZPACHO

This is a popular Spanish soup with a delicate but pungent flavor. It should be served very cold and in small portions (it will definitely serve six).

¾ cup blanched almonds
4 large garlic cloves, chopped
4 ounces unbleached white bread,
  crusts removed
About 2½ cups non-carbonated
  mineral water
½ cup extra-virgin olive oil,
  plus extra to garnish

1 tablespoon sherry vinegar
Salt
12 ounces Muscat grapes, peeled,
  halved, and seeds removed
6 ice cubes
Paprika, for dusting

Place the almonds, garlic, and bread in a food processor and process until it forms a paste, adding a little of the water if necessary to move the mixture around. Gradually add the oil, vinegar, and enough of the remaining water to make a smooth soup. Season to taste with salt.

Pour into a bowl and cover tightly with plastic wrap. Chill for at least 2 hours; overnight is best. Remove from the refrigerator, give a good stir, and correct the seasoning and adjust the consistency as necessary with a little more water. Fold in the grapes. Ladle into small, colorful bowls and add an ice cube and a drizzle of the olive oil to each portion. Sprinkle over a little paprika and serve ice cold.

LIGHT & HEALTHY

When you come home late after work or an evening out, a full-scale dinner is often out of the question, but a light and wholesome bowl of soup can just fit the bill. These are recipes low in fat but high on flavor. You will find that a diet that revolves around soup is not only a healthy diet, but also can be a perfect solution for anyone who wants to lose weight. All recipes serve 4 to 6.

CARROT AND GINGER SOUP

This is not only cheap and easy to make, but it has a fantastic vibrant color. What more could you want?

1 tablespoon sunflower oil	1 tablespoon honey
1 large onion, minced	1/2 lemon, seeds removed
2 tablespoons freshly grated gingerroot	Salt and freshly ground black pepper
6 cups grated carrots	

Heat the oil in a large saucepan. Add the onion and ginger and cook over low heat for 10 minutes until soft but not brown.

Stir in the carrots, honey, and a squeeze of lemon juice. Pour in 3³⁄₄ cups water and bring to a boil. Lower the heat and simmer for 40 minutes, or until the carrots are soft and the soup has thickened.

Purée the soup in batches in a food processor or with a hand-held blender. To serve, reheat slowly and season to taste. Ladle into bowls and add a grind of black pepper to serve.

RED PEPPER AND TOMATO SOUP

Lovely to eat at any time of the year, this soup is, however, best at the end of the summer when tomatoes are plentiful and cheap. If you can't find any decent ones, replace the quantity below with one can (14-oz.) crushed tomatoes in rich tomato juice. Or, use 2 cups *passata di pomodoro* (finely strained tomato sauce sold in jars in gourmet shops).

1 tablespoon olive oil	2 large red bell peppers, seeded and chopped
6 scallions, minced, with white and green parts separated	Salt and freshly ground black pepper
3 cups peeled, seeded, and chopped ripe tomatoes	3³⁄₄ cups vegetable or chicken stock
	Pinch of sugar
	4 to 6 tablespoons low-fat yogurt or fromage blanc

Heat the olive oil in a large saucepan. Add the white parts of the scallions and cook for a minute or so. Add the tomatoes and peppers and cook for 5 minutes longer, or until tender. Season generously. Pour in the stock and bring to a boil. Lower the heat and simmer for 10 minutes until reduced and thickened slightly.

Purée in batches in a food processor or with a hand-held blender. Pour back into a clean saucepan and stir in the green part of the scallions and the sugar. Season to taste and reheat slowly. Ladle into bowls and garnish with a spoonful of the yogurt or fromage blanc. Add a good grind of black pepper to serve.

CUCUMBER AND YOGURT SOUP

This refreshing and delicious combination is great for hot days or as a soup course during a spicy meal to help cleanse the palate.

2 cucumbers, peeled, seeded, and chopped	8 drops hot-pepper sauce
1 teaspoon fine sea salt	2 tablespoons chopped mixed fresh chives, dill, mint, tarragon, and flat-leaf parsley
1¹⁄₄ cups chicken stock	Salt and freshly ground black pepper
2¹⁄₂ cups thick plain yogurt	Salsa fresca (page 12), to garnish
2⁄₃ cup sour cream	

Place the cucumber in a colander and sprinkle the salt over; set aside for 30 minutes. Rinse well under cold water and squeeze out the excess moisture in a clean dish towel.

Place the cucumber in a food processor with the stock, yogurt, sour cream, hot-pepper sauce, herbs, and plenty of seasoning. Process to a purée; you may have to do this in batches. Pour into a large bowl and cover with plastic wrap. Chill for at least 2 hours; overnight is best.

Remove the soup from the refrigerator and stir. Season to taste and ladle into bowls. Scatter some salsa fresca over and serve ice cold.

SPICY WINTER VEGETABLE SOUP

Substitute pumpkin, rutabaga, or turnip for the parsnips and carrots, or just use a mixture—this is a very flexible recipe.

1 tablespoon olive oil	1 tablespoon medium curry powder or paste
2 small leeks, thinly sliced	3³⁄₄ cups vegetable stock
2¹⁄₂ cups diced parsnips	Salt and freshly ground black pepper
1¹⁄₂ cups diced carrots	2⁄₃ cup 2 percent milk
1 cup diced potato	Toasted cumin seeds, to garnish

Heat the oil in a large saucepan. Add the vegetables and cook for 1 minute or so until well coated. Lower the heat, cover, and cook for about 10 minutes, stirring occasionally until soft but not colored. Stir in the curry powder or paste and cook for another minute or so, stirring.

Pour in the stock, season to taste, and bring to a boil. Lower the heat and simmer for 25 to 30 minutes until the vegetables are tender and the liquid has reduced slightly. Remove from the heat and leave to cool a little. Purée in batches in a food processor or with a hand-held blender. Return to a clean saucepan and stir in the milk. Reheat slowly until just warm, without boiling. Ladle into bowls and garnish with toasted cumin seeds. Serve at once.

Beet Borscht

"Borscht" or "borshch" is a general name for a number of Eastern European beet soups that vary a great deal—this version, however, is my favorite.

1 tablespoon olive oil
1 large leek, minced
2 celery sticks, minced
4 cups peeled and finely grated beets
1 potato, grated
2 cups finely grated carrots

3³⁄4 cups vegetable or chicken stock
1 tablespoon red wine vinegar
1 teaspoon sugar
Salt and freshly ground black pepper
About 2 tablespoons sour cream (optional)

Heat the oil in a large saucepan. Add the leek and celery and fry for about 5 minutes until soft. Add the beets, potato, and most of the carrots, reserving some for garnish. Pour in the stock and bring to a boil. Lower the heat and simmer for 40 minutes, or until the vegetables are tender and the soup has thickened slightly.

Stir in the vinegar and sugar and season to taste. To serve, ladle into bowls and garnish with a small spoonful of sour cream, if using, and a little grated carrot.

Oyster and Leek Soup

This special soup with a spicy kick has fresh oysters added at the last minute. It is the perfect appetizer for a romantic meal.

1 tablespoon olive oil
4 large shallots, minced
1 mild red chili, seeded and minced
3³⁄4 cups fish stock
4 small leeks, thinly sliced

24 oysters, opened and loosened (with juices reserved)
1 heaping teaspoon chopped fresh chervil
Salt and freshly ground black pepper
¹⁄2 lemon, seeds removed

Heat the oil in a large saucepan. Add the shallots and chili and cook slowly for about 5 minutes until soft. Pour in the stock and bring to a boil. Lower the heat and simmer for 5 minutes, or until the flavors combine.

Add the leeks and simmer for 2 minutes longer until they are just tender, but still bright green. Add the oysters and strain in their juice through a fine strainer to remove any of the little pieces of shell. Stir in the chervil and season to taste. Bring to a slow simmer to just barely poach the oysters. Remove from the heat and add a squeeze of lemon juice to taste.

Divide the oysters between serving bowls and ladle the remaining broth over. Serve at once with a glass of chilled champagne. Enjoy!

Spring Pea Soup

You don't have to use fresh peas for this soup, because frozen work just as well, but the flavors are all colorful and vibrant, hence the name.

3 cups shelled fresh or frozen peas
Juice of 1 lime
2 heaping tablespoons fresh basil leaves plus extra to garnish
2 mild red chilies, seeded and finely chopped
¹⁄2 teaspoon ground cumin
¹⁄2 teaspoon ground coriander
Good pinch paprika, plus extra to garnish

Salt and freshly ground black pepper
1 tablespoon olive oil
6 scallions, minced
1 garlic clove, crushed
3³⁄4 cups vegetable stock
2 ripe plum tomatoes, peeled, seeded, and diced
Lime-infused yogurt (page 16), to garnish (optional)

Place the peas in a saucepan of boiling salted water and cook for 4 to 5 minutes until just tender. Drain and refresh under cold water.

Place the lime juice in a food processor with the fresh basil and chilies and process until smooth. Add the peas with the ground cumin, coriander, paprika, and plenty of seasoning. Process again until smooth.

Heat the oil in a large saucepan. Add the scallions and garlic and cook for 1 to 2 minutes, stirring. Add the pea mixture and and slowly pour in the stock, stirring. Stir in the tomatoes, bring to a simmer, and just heat through.

Season to taste and remove the soup from the heat. Ladle into bowls and add a spoonful of the lime-infused yogurt, if desired. Garnish with a sprinkling of paprika and some torn basil leaves. Serve at once.

Above: Beet Borscht

Watercress and Apple Soup

The natural sweetness of the apples gives this soup a wonderful flavor. It can be served warm or ice cold, depending on the season.

1 tablespoon olive oil
2 leeks, thinly sliced
2 bunches fresh watercress
3 apples, peeled, cored, and diced
1/2 lemon, seeds removed

1 cup peeled and diced potato
3 3/4 cups chicken or vegetable stock
Salt and freshly ground black pepper
2/3 cup thick plain yogurt

Heat the oil in a saucepan. Add the leeks and cook for about 5 minutes until soft but not brown. Chop the watercress, separating the leaves and stems. Add the watercress stems to the leeks with most of the apples, reserving some for garnish, and a squeeze of the lemon juice to stop the apples from turning brown. Add the potato, cover, and cook slowly for 10 minutes until the potato is just tender but not brown, stirring occasionally.

Pour in the stock, season to taste, and bring to a boil. Lower the heat and simmer for 20 minutes until the apples and potato are soft and the soup has thickened slightly. Add the reserved watercress leaves, keeping some back for garnish, and simmer for 1 minute. Remove the pan from the heat.

Purée the soup in batches in a food processor or with a hand-held blender. Pour back into a clean pan and whisk in the yogurt, then season to taste and add an additional squeeze of lemon juice to taste. Reheat slowly to warm through; do not boil. Ladle into bowls and garnish with the reserved apple and watercress leaves. Serve at once.

Sorrel Soup

Sorrel is a soft, leafy green herb that has a sharp, almost lemony flavor. It keeps very well in a plastic bag in the salad drawer of the refrigerator. If, however, you can't find any, use tender, young spinach leaves instead.

1 tablespoon olive oil
1 onion, minced
1 large garlic clove, crushed
1 bay leaf
1 1/2 cups peeled and diced potatoes

2 celery sticks, diced
3 3/4 cups vegetable stock
2 ounces sorrel leaves
Salt and freshly ground black pepper

Heat the oil in a large saucepan. Add the onion, garlic, and bay leaf and cook for about 5 minutes until soft but not colored. Add the potatoes and celery and cook for 1 to 2 minutes longer, stirring.

Pour in the stock and bring to a boil. Lower the heat and simmer for 15 to 20 minutes until the vegetables are tender.

Add the sorrel and cook for another minute, stirring constantly. Remove the bay leaf and purée the soup in batches in a food processor or with a hand-held blender. Pour back into a clean saucepan, season to taste, and reheat slowly. Ladle into bowls and add a good grind of black pepper to serve.

Above: *Quick Gazpacho*

Quick Gazpacho

It is worth remembering when making this soup that cold food needs to be highly seasoned to bring out the best flavors.

3 3/4 cups tomato juice
1 red bell pepper, seeded and chopped
1 red onion, chopped
1 small cucumber, peeled, seeded, and
  chopped
1 garlic clove, chopped

Handful fresh basil leaves, plus extra
  to garnish
1 tablespoon extra-virgin olive oil
1 tablespoon red wine vinegar
1 teaspoon sugar
Salt and freshly ground black pepper

Place the tomato juice, red pepper, onion, cucumber, garlic, basil, olive oil, vinegar, and sugar in a food processor and blend to a smooth purée—you may have to do this in batches. Season to taste and chill until very cold.

To serve, ladle into bowls and shred the remaining basil leaves on top to garnish.

GREEN SUMMER SOUP

This is fabulous on a hot summer's day. If your diet allows, garnish each serving with a frozen olive oil cube, made in an ice cube tray.

1 small cucumber, peeled, seeded, and minced
Salt and freshly ground black pepper
1¼ cups low-fat plain yogurt
⅔ cup tomato juice
4 scallions, minced

1 small garlic clove, crushed
2 cups vegetable stock
2 tablespoons shredded fresh mint, plus extra to garnish
Few drops hot-pepper sauce

Place the cucumber in a colander and sprinkle with 1 teaspoon salt; set aside to drain for 30 minutes. Rinse under cold water and squeeze out any excess moisture with a clean dish towel.

Place the yogurt, tomato juice, scallions, garlic, stock, and mint in a food processor and blend to a smooth purée—you may have to do this in batches. Stir in the cucumber and hot-pepper sauce. Season to taste and chill until very cold. To serve, ladle into bowls and garnish with the remaining mint.

GARLIC PURÉE SOUP

This great winter warmer packs a subtle smoky garlic punch. You don't have to add the fromage blanc if you're watching the calories, in which case use a little extra stock to thin the soup.

1 garlic bulb, unpeeled and separated into cloves
1 tablespoon olive oil
2 onions, minced
1 heaping teaspoon chopped rosemary needles
2½ cups diced potatoes

2½ cups peeled, seeded, and chopped ripe tomatoes
3¾ cups chicken stock
1¼ cups low-fat fromage blanc
Salt and freshly ground black pepper
2 teaspoons snipped fresh chives

Preheat the oven to 400°F. Place the garlic cloves in a very small roasting pan and roast for 25 to 30 minutes until lightly charred and tender; leave to cool completely.

Heat the oil in a large saucepan. Add the onions, rosemary, and potatoes and cook for about 5 minutes until soft. Add the tomatoes, pour in the stock, and cover, simmering for 20 minutes, or until the potatoes are tender. Peel the garlic cloves and stir into the soup; leave to cool a little.

Purée the soup in batches in a food processor or with a hand-held blender. Return to the pan and stir in the fromage blanc, reserving some to garnish.

Season the soup to taste and reheat slowly; do not boil. Ladle into bowls and add spoonfuls of the reserved fromage blanc. Add a good grind of black pepper and sprinkle the chives on top to serve.

SPANISH-STYLE MUSSEL SOUP

This soup has a wonderful rich flavor and you would never notice it only uses one tablespoon of oil.

4½ pounds fresh mussels, cleaned
1¼ cups dry white wine
3 large garlic cloves, peeled and halved
Salt and freshly ground black pepper
Good pinch saffron strands soaked in 1 tablespoon hot water
1 tablespoon olive oil
1 large onion, chopped

2½ cups peeled, seeded, and chopped ripe tomatoes
2½ cups fish stock
2 slices unbleached white bread, toasted and cubed
½ teaspoon cayenne pepper
2 tablespoons flat-leaf parsley leaves
3 tablespoons brandy

Discard any cracked or opened mussels that do not close when tapped. Place the wine and 2 of the garlic cloves in a large saucepan, season with pepper, and bring to a boil. Add the saffron and mussels, cover, and cook over high heat for 2 to 3 minutes, shaking the pan occasionally, until they just open—discard any that don't. Drain, reserving the cooking liquid, and discard the garlic. When the mussels are cool enough to handle, remove the shells, reserving some of the nicest looking whole mussels for a garnish.

Heat the oil in the saucepan. Add the onion and cook for about 15 minutes until soft and golden, stirring occasionally. Add the tomatoes and cook for another few minutes until soft but still holding their color. Pour in the stock and strain in the reserved mussel cooking liquid through a double layer of cheesecloth to remove any sand and grit. Bring to a simmer.

Place the remaining garlic in a mini-blender with the toast, cayenne pepper, parsley, and brandy. Blend to a smooth paste, adding a little of the stock if necessary to help the mixture move around. Stir into the soup and cook for about 1 minute until thick. Add the mussels, season to taste, and just heat through without boiling. Ladle into bowls and garnish with the reserved whole mussels to serve.

Right: Green Summer Soup

ROASTED YELLOW PEPPER SOUP

Broiled peppers have the most wonderful, smoky sweetness, which I just adore. Collect as much of the juices as possible as you peel them, because they really have a fantastic flavor.

4 yellow bell peppers	1 potato, diced
1 tablespoon olive oil	1 teaspoon chopped fresh oregano
1 onion, minced	3³/4 cups vegetable or chicken stock
2 garlic cloves, minced	Salt and freshly ground black pepper
1 red chili, seeded and minced	

Heat the broiler. Place the peppers on the broiler rack and broil for 20 to 30 minutes until the skins are charred and blistered, turning frequently. Transfer to a plastic bag, secure with a knot, and leave the peppers to steam in their own heat for 10 minutes. Remove from the bag, and peel, seed, and chop the flesh, reserving any juices.

Heat the oil in a large saucepan. Add the onion, garlic, and chili and cook for about 10 minutes until soft but not brown. Add the peppers with their juices, along with the potato, oregano, and stock and bring to a boil. Lower the heat and simmer for about 30 minutes until the potato is tender and the soup is thicker. Leave the soup to cool a little.

Purée in batches in a food processor or with a hand-held blender. To serve, reheat slowly and season to taste. Ladle into bowls and add a grind of black pepper to serve.

CHICKEN CONSOMMÉ

If chilled, this consommé will develop a gelled texture. If you want to serve it like this, just break it up with a fork and spoon into small, pretty cups. Garnish with plenty of chopped fresh herbs and you've got a soup fit for a king!

1¹/2 quarts chicken stock	2 egg whites, lightly beaten
3 cups chopped ripe tomatoes	2 egg shells, crushed
1 large onion, chopped	Pinch of sugar
2 celery sticks, chopped	Dash of Madeira (optional)
2 carrots, chopped	Salt and freshly ground black pepper
1 bouquet garni	Vegetable hair (page 15), to garnish,
10 ounces lean ground chicken	(optional)

Place the stock in a large saucepan with the tomatoes, onion, celery, carrots, and bouquet garni and bring to a boil. Lower the heat and simmer for 25 to 30 minutes until the vegetables are soft.

Stir the ground chicken into the stock, stirring until well blended. Add the egg whites and shells. Return to a boil, whisking continuously. Lower the heat and simmer for 30 minutes longer.

Strain the soup through a cheesecloth-lined fine strainer and return to a clean pan. Season to taste and add the sugar and Madeira, if using. Ladle into bowls and garnish with small mounds of vegetable hair, if your diet allows.

PROVENÇAL SWEET PEPPER SOUP

This is a variation on the fiery, hot Provençal rouille sauce, traditionally served with fish soups. If you don't want to use heavy cream in the yellow pepper cream, replace it with thick plain yogurt—the contrast of colors is very dramatic.

4 large red bell peppers	¹/2 teaspoon caraway seeds
2 slices day-old unbleached white bread	¹/4 teaspoon each cumin and coriander seeds
2 large garlic cloves, crushed	1 tablespoon olive oil
2 red bird's-eye chilies, seeded and chopped	3³/4 cups vegetable stock
Good handful fresh basil leaves	Yellow pepper cream (page 16), to garnish
Salt and freshly ground black pepper	(optional)

Heat the broiler. Place the peppers on the broiler rack and broil for 20 to 30 minutes until charred and blistered, turning regularly. Place in a plastic bag, secure with a knot, and leave the peppers to steam in their own heat for 10 minutes. Remove from the bag, and peel, seed, and chop the flesh, reserving any juices.

Meanwhile, soak the bread in a little water for about 5 minutes. Squeeze out the excess moisture. Place in a food processor with the pepper and any juices, the garlic, chilies, and basil. Season generously and process to a purée.

Place the caraway, cumin, and coriander seeds in a mortar and crush to a fine powder with a pestle. Heat the oil in a large saucepan. Stir in the ground spices and cook for 30 seconds, stirring. Pour in the stock and whisk in the pepper mixture until well combined. Season to taste and bring to a simmer to warm through. Ladle into bowls, add a good grind of black pepper, and serve topped with spoonfuls of yellow pepper cream, if desired.

VIRGIN MARY SOUP

I love this soup scattered with guacamole.

1 tablespoon olive oil	3 tablespoons Worcestershire sauce
3 cups roughly chopped tomatoes,	3 tablespoons balsamic vinegar
or 2 cups passata di pomodoro	Juice of 2 limes
(finely strained tomato sauce	12 drops hot-pepper sauce
sold in gourmet shops)	Celery salt and freshly ground black pepper
4 scallions, minced	12 to 18 small ice cubes
3³/4 cups tomato juice, preferably	Guacamole (page 15), to garnish (optional)
freshly squeezed	

Place the oil in a food processor. Add the tomatoes, scallions, tomato juice, Worcestershire sauce, balsamic vinegar, lime juice, hot-pepper sauce, and plenty of celery salt and freshly ground black pepper. Process until smooth—you may have to do this in batches—and pass through a fine strainer into a large bowl.

Cover the bowl with plastic wrap and chill for at least 2 hours; overnight is best. Ladle the soup into bowls and add a couple of ice cubes to each one. Scatter the guacamole over, if using, and serve ice cold.

Right: Roasted Yellow Pepper Soup

FAST & EASY

These days, who has time to be stuck in the kitchen for hours preparing food? The recipes in this chapter have been devised with the busy cook in mind—all can be made in less than half an hour, some take far less. The ingredients have been kept to a minimum and you may already have many of these things, with the recipes requiring mostly cans and frozen foods. All recipes serve 4 to 6.

LETTUCE SOUP

This is a fantastic summer soup, but remember your finished soup will only taste as good as the lettuce you use. Buy it as fresh as possible for the best sweet, delicate flavor.

3 tablespoons unsalted butter
2 shallots, minced
1 large romaine or butterhead lettuce, core removed and leaves finely shredded
4 teaspoons finely chopped fresh tarragon

Salt and freshly ground black pepper
3¾ cups vegetable stock
⅔ cup heavy cream
2 egg yolks

Melt the butter in a large saucepan. Add the shallots and cook gently for about 5 minutes until soft but not colored. Stir in the lettuce and half of the tarragon and season generously. Cover and cook slowly for 3 to 4 minutes, shaking the pan occasionally, until the lettuce wilts.

Pour the stock into the pan and quickly bring to a boil. Lower the heat and simmer for another 5 minutes.

Mix the cream and egg yolks together in a bowl. Add a ladleful of the hot soup and mix well to combine, then whisk back into the soup. Return to low heat and cook for another minute or so until just heated through. Stir in the remaining tarragon and ladle into bowls to serve.

MIXED SEAFOOD SOUP

This is actually a bit of a cheat I've learned from the restaurant trade—apparently nobody ever notices . . .You can use any type of fish soup as the base, but obviously the better brands give the better result.

2 cans (14-oz.) fish soup
3¾ cups store-bought fish stock, or stock made with a cube or granules
Pinch saffron strands soaked in 1 tablespoon hot water

1 pound mixed prepared seafood, such as shelled mussels, cooked shelled shrimp, and squid rings, thawed if frozen
4 tablespoons brandy
Salt and freshly ground black pepper
Garlic croutons (page 14 or store-bought), to serve

Place the fish soup in a saucepan with the stock, saffron, and mixed seafood. Stir in the brandy and season to taste—you'll probably find you need to go easy on the salt.

Bring to a boil. Lower the heat and simmer for about 5 minutes until heated through. Ladle into bowls and garnish with garlic croutons to serve—it's as simple as that!

SPRING ZUCCHINI SOUP

If you use the grating blade on a food processor to grate the zucchini, the preparation time for this soup will cut down to less than a minute. I like to make this in the spring when there is an abundance of herbs growing on my windowsill, but it's great at any time of year.

2 tablespoons olive oil
1 onion, minced
6 cups grated zucchini
Salt and freshly ground black pepper

3¾ cups vegetable stock
4 tablespoons chopped fresh mixed chives, flat-leaf parsley, tarragon, and chervil
Parmesan croûtes (page 14), to garnish

Heat the oil in a large saucepan. Add the onion and cook for a few minutes until soft but not colored. Stir in the zucchini, season generously, cover, and cook slowly for 5 minutes until just tender.

Uncover, pour in the stock, and bring to a boil. Reduce the heat, cover once more, and simmer for 10 minutes longer, or until just tender.

Stir in the herbs and purée in a food processor or with a hand-held blender. Return to the saucepan, season to taste, and reheat slowly without boiling. Ladle into bowls and garnish with Parmesan croûtes to serve.

CHILI–BEAN SOUP

For an authentic Mexican flavor, either garnish the soup bowls with spoonfuls of sour cream and a sprinkling of grated cheddar, or pile tiny mounds of guacamole (page 15) onto tortilla chips and serve them alongside or float them on top.

2 tablespoons sunflower oil
1 red onion, minced
½ teaspoon each ground cumin, coriander, and paprika
2 zucchini, cut into small pieces
1 cup baby corn, cut into small pieces

1 can (14-oz.) mixed beans, drained and rinsed
1 can (14-oz.) crushed tomatoes
2 tablespoons bottled chili and garlic sauce
2½ cups vegetable stock
Salt and freshly ground black pepper

Heat the oil in a large saucepan. Add the onion and fry for a few minutes until soft. Add the ground cumin, coriander, and paprika and cook for another minute, stirring. Add the zucchini and corn and stir-fry for 1 to 2 minutes until combined.

Add the beans, tomatoes, chili and garlic sauce, and stock and bring to a boil. Lower the heat and simmer for 6 to 8 minutes until slightly thickened. Season to taste and ladle into small bowls. Serve hot.

PEPERONATA SOUP

This is a version of the traditional Italian stew of peppers and tomatoes. To make this recipe even quicker, blend a couple of jars of mixed pepper antipasto with an equal quantity of stock.

4 tablespoons extra-virgin olive oil	2 1/2 cups vegetable or chicken stock
1 large onion, minced	Salt and freshly ground black pepper
2 red and 2 yellow bell peppers, seeded and chopped	Good pinch of sugar
2 garlic cloves, crushed	1 teaspoon white-wine vinegar
1 can (14-oz.) crushed tomatoes in rich tomato juice	Deep-fried basil leaves (page 15), to garnish (optional)

Heat the oil in a large saucepan. Add the onion and peppers and cook over fairly high heat for about 10 minutes until just tender and beginning to color around the edges, stirring occasionally. Stir in the garlic and cook for 1 to 2 minutes longer, stirring occasionally. Tip in the tomatoes and stock. Season to taste and bring to a boil. Lower the heat and simmer for 10 to 15 minutes until the peppers are tender.

Purée in batches in a food processor or with a hand-held blender. Return to a clean saucepan, stir in the sugar and vinegar, and season to taste. Reheat slowly. Ladle into bowls and garnish with the basil leaves, if using.

BAKED BEAN SOUP

Even if the title of this soup sounds a bit strange, I can assure you kids love it. I made it up one day when I was unexpectedly left with a bunch of children (the person responsible shall remain nameless) and it was a great success.

1 pound pork link sausages	1 can (14-oz.) baked beans
2 tablespoons sunflower oil	2 teaspoons Worcestershire sauce
1 large onion	Salt and freshly ground black pepper
3 3/4 cups vegetable stock (stock from a cube is fine)	Toasted cheese croûtes (page 14), to garnish

Heat the broiler. Arrange the sausages on the broiler rack and broil for a few minutes on each side until cooked through and lightly brown. Leave until cool enough to handle, then cut into small pieces.

Heat the oil in a large saucepan. Add the onion and cook for 5 minutes, or until soft and light brown around the edges. Stir in the sausages.

Pour the stock into the saucepan. Add the beans and Worcestershire sauce, season to taste, and bring to a boil. Lower the heat and simmer for about 5 minutes until heated through. Ladle the soup into bowls and top each one with 3 toasted cheese croûtes to serve.

SHRIMP AND CUCUMBER SOUP

You don't even need an oven to make this soup. If you've got the time it's worth sprinkling the cucumber with salt—set it aside for about 15 minutes, then rinse under cold running water, and squeeze dry in a clean dish towel. This technique removes excess water and firms up the flesh.

8 ounces cooked, shelled shrimp, ground, plus 4 to 6 whole ones, to garnish	1 1/4 cups non-carbonated mineral water
1 cucumber, halved, seeded, and grated, plus 8 to 12 wafer-thin slices, to garnish	2 1/2 cups plain yogurt
2 tablespoons chopped fresh dill, plus plus 4 to 6 tiny sprigs, to garnish	Salt and freshly ground black pepper

Place the shrimp and cucumber in a large bowl and season generously. Stir in the dill and pour in the water and yogurt, stirring until well combined. Cover with plastic wrap and chill for at least 2 hours; overnight is best. (Or start with all the ingredients well chilled and serve it straight away.)

When you are ready to serve, remove the plastic wrap and give the soup a good stir. Season to taste and ladle into bowls. Garnish each bowl with 2 cucumber slices, slightly overlapping and topped with a shrimp and a tiny dill sprig. Serve ice cold.

FIELD MUSHROOM SOUP

This soup doesn't take much longer than 20 minutes to make from start to finish. I find the lemon juice helps bring out the mushrooms' natural, savory flavor. If you are trying to eat healthily, omit the cream and dilute the soup with a little extra stock if necessary—you'll find it's still pretty good.

1 1/2 pounds large, flat mushrooms, chopped	2 tablespoons all-purpose flour
Juice of 1/2 lemon	3 3/4 cups vegetable stock
4 tablespoons unsalted butter	Pinch of freshly grated nutmeg
1 onion, chopped	Salt and freshly ground black pepper
1 large garlic clove, crushed	2/3 cup heavy cream

Sprinkle the mushrooms with the lemon juice. Melt the butter in a large saucepan. Add the onion and garlic and cook gently for a few minutes until soft but not colored. Increase the heat, add the mushrooms, and cook for 1 to 2 minutes, stirring. Stir in the flour and cook for another minute, stirring.

Gradually pour the stock into the pan. Add the nutmeg, season to taste, and bring to a boil. Lower the heat, cover, and simmer for 10 minutes, or until the mushrooms are tender. Purée in a food processor or with a hand-held blender. Return to a clean saucepan, season to taste, and stir in the most of the cream, reserving a little to garnish. Reheat slowly; do not boil. Ladle into bowls and add swirls of the reserved cream. Serve at once.

Right: Peperonata Soup

GARBANZO AND GARLIC SOUP

This is a rich, intensely spicy soup that reminds me of Moroccan vacations. It is made almost entirely from kitchen pantry ingredients.

4 tablespoons extra-virgin olive oil, plus extra to garnish
1 large onion, minced
2 large garlic cloves, minced
1 heaping teaspoon ground cumin
2 cans (14-oz.) garbanzo beans, drained and rinsed

3³/₄ cups vegetable or vegetable stock
Salt and freshly ground black pepper
4 tablespoons chopped fresh cilantro, plus extra leaves, to garnish
Few drops hot-pepper sauce
Juice of ¹/₂ lemon

Heat the oil in a large saucepan. Add the onion and garlic. Cook for about 5 minutes until very soft but not brown. Stir in the cumin and cook for a minute or so, stirring. Add the garbanzo beans and pour in the stock. Season generously and bring to a boil. Lower the heat and simmer for 10 minutes, or until the flavors are combined.

Place half of the soup in a food processor with the cilantro and process to a purée. Return to the saucepan and stir until well combined. Heat through, add the hot-pepper sauce and lemon juice, and season to taste. Ladle into bowls and garnish with swirls of olive oil and cilantro leaves.

AVGOLEMONO SOUP

I first tasted this while on vacation in Greece and wasn't sure whether I liked it. Over the years, however, it has really grown on me and now it's one of the first things I want when I get off the plane.

2 tablespoons olive oil
6 scallions, minced, with white and green parts separated
8 ounces boneless, skinless chicken breast halves, cut into strips
¹/₂ cup long-grain rice

5 cups chicken stock
Salt and freshly ground black pepper
2 eggs
Juice of 1 lemon
1 tablespoon finely chopped fresh flat-leaf parsley

Heat the oil in a large saucepan. Add the white parts of the scallions and stir-fry for 20 seconds. Add the chicken and stir-fry for 3 to 4 minutes longer, stirring frequently until the chicken is sealed and lightly golden.

Stir in the rice and stock, season to taste, and bring to a boil. Lower the heat and simmer for 10 to 12 minutes until the rice is tender.

Meanwhile, beat the eggs in a bowl with the lemon juice. When the rice is tender, reduce the heat to as low as possible and whisk in the egg mixture. Simmer over very low heat for 1 to 2 minutes, whisking continuously until the egg is just cooked but not rubbery.

Remove the soup from the heat, season to taste, and stir in the parsley. Ladle into bowls and scatter the green parts of the scallions on top to serve.

BROCCOLI AND CHEDDAR SOUP

My mom used to make this all the time when we were young. We'd get a big bowl as soon as we got in from school on a cold winter's evening to keep us going until our dinner.

3 tablespoons unsalted butter
1 large onion, minced
1¹/₂ cups peeled and finely diced potatoes
Salt and freshly ground black pepper

3³/₄ cups vegetable stock
1 broccoli head, about ¹/₂ pound, well trimmed and finely chopped
1¹/₄ cups finely grated cheddar cheese

Melt the butter in a large saucepan. Add the onion and cook for a few minutes until soft. Stir in the potato and season generously. Cover and cook slowly for 10 minutes, shaking the pan occasionally, until the potatoes are just tender.

Pour the stock into the pan and bring to a boil. Lower the heat, add the broccoli, and simmer for 5 minutes, or until the broccoli is just tender.

Purée in batches in a food processor or with a hand-held blender. Return to a clean pan and stir in the cheddar. Reheat over low heat for 1 to 2 minutes until just warmed through. Season to taste and ladle into bowls. Serve at once.

Above: Garbanzo and Garlic Soup

WINTER VEGETABLE SOUP

This has to be one of easiest and most versatile soups I know—you don't even need to use any stock as the flavors are already powerful enough. You can vary the combination of vegetables you use, just keep the final weight to 1½ pounds, or about 5 cups.

4 tablespoons unsalted butter	1 small parsnip, grated
1 onion, minced	1 small potato, peeled and grated
2 small leeks, minced	1 tablespoon honey
1 heaping tablespoon grated fresh gingerroot	3¾ cups boiling water
Salt and freshly ground black pepper	½ lemon, seeds removed
3 cups grated carrots	

Melt the butter in a large saucepan. Add the onion, leeks, and ginger, season generously, cover, and cook slowly for 2 to 3 minutes until soft. Stir in the carrots, parsnip, potato, and honey. Cover again and continue cooking for 5 minutes until soft.

Pour the water into the pan and return to a boil. Lower the heat and simmer for 8 to 10 minutes longer until all the vegetables are tender.

Purée the soup in a food processor or with a hand-held blender. Return to a clean saucepan and season to taste. Add a squeeze of lemon juice and reheat slowly. Ladle into bowls and serve at once.

POTATO AND LEEK SOUP

You can now buy small, pencil-sized leeks, often in the organic section of supermarkets. I think they have an excellent flavor and always seem to be less dirty, so keep a look out for them.

4 tablespoons unsalted butter	Salt and freshly ground pepper
3 cups finely sliced leeks	3¾ cups chicken stock
1½ cups peeled and diced potatoes	⅔ cup heavy cream
1 heaping teaspoon fresh thyme leaves, plus extra to garnish	

Melt the butter in a large saucepan. As soon as it foams, stir in the leeks and potatoes and stir until well coated. Add the thyme and season generously. Press a buttered circle of parchment paper on top of the vegetables, cover the pan with a tight-fitting lid, and cook over low heat for about 10 minutes, shaking the pan occasionally, until the vegetables are soft but not colored.

Remove the lid and paper from the pan. Pour in the stock and bring to a boil. Lower the heat and simmer for about 5 minutes until the potatoes are tender.

Purée the soup in batches in a food processor or with a hand-held blender. Pour back into a clean saucepan, season to taste and add the cream. Reheat slowly; do not boil. Ladle into bowls and garnish with thyme leaves. Serve at once.

Above: Mexican Avocado Soup

MEXICAN AVOCADO SOUP

This is a superb cold soup, which is excellent eaten with salsa fresca (page 12) piled in tiny mounds onto hot and spicy tortilla chips.

4 large, ripe avocados	Grated zest and juice of 1 lime
6 scallions, chopped	2 cups vegetable or chicken stock
2 garlic cloves, chopped	Fine sea salt and freshly ground black pepper
1 large green chili, seeded and chopped	
2 tablespoons chopped fresh cilantro, plus extra leaves to garnish	1¼ cups plain yogurt
	⅔ cup sour cream

Halve the avocados, remove the pits, and scoop out the flesh. Place in a food processor with the scallions, garlic, chili, cilantro, lime zest and juice, and stock. Season generously and process to a purée. Transfer to a large bowl and stir in the yogurt and most of the sour cream.

Cover with plastic wrap and chill until very cold.

To serve, give the soup a good stir and season to taste. Ladle into bowls. Garnish with small spoonfuls of the remaining sour cream, seasoning to taste, and the cilantro leaves. Serve at once.

PEA AND MINT SOUP

This soup is about as instant as you are ever going to get. It is good served both hot and cold, and the addition of the chili gives it a surprising and pleasant kick.

4 tablespoons unsalted butter
1 onion, minced
2 garlic cloves, crushed
1 green chili, seeded and minced
3 cups frozen peas
Pinch of sugar

3¾ cups vegetable or chicken stock
Salt and freshly ground black pepper
2 tablespoons chopped fresh mint, plus
    extra leaves to garnish
Softly whipped cream, to garnish

Melt the butter in a large saucepan. Add the onion, garlic, and chili and cook for 3 to 4 minutes until soft but not colored. Add the peas, sugar, and stock. Season generously and bring to a boil. Lower the heat and simmer for 8 minutes until the peas are tender.

Add the mint to the soup. Purée in a food processor or with a hand-held blender. To serve, reheat slowly and season to taste. Ladle into bowls and add swirls of cream and mint leaves to garnish.

CREAM OF SPINACH SOUP

Impressive enough to grace any dinner-party table, this soup can be made in the time it takes your guests to have a drink. You could also make it with a bag of frozen spinach and just cook it for a bit longer at the beginning.

2 tablespoons olive oil
1 garlic clove, crushed
1 pound tender, young spinach
Salt and freshly ground black pepper
Pinch freshly grated nutmeg
3¾ cups vegetable stock

⅔ cup heavy cream
2 egg yolks
6 tablespoons freshly grated Parmesan
Bacon croutons (page 14), to garnish
    (optional)

Heat the oil in a large saucepan. Add the garlic and stir-fry for 20 seconds. Tip in the spinach and press it down well. Season generously and add the nutmeg. Cover and cook for a few minutes, shaking the pan occasionally, until the spinach wilts.

Pour the stock into the saucepan and bring to a boil. Lower the heat and simmer for 2 to 3 minutes until all the flavors are combined; leave to cool a little.

Purée in batches in a food processor or with a hand-held blender. Return to the saucepan off the heat and season to taste.

Mix together the cream and egg yolks in a bowl and beat in the Parmesan. Add a ladleful of the hot soup and stir together, then whisk back into the soup. Return to low heat and cook for another minute or so until just heated through; do not boil. Ladle into bowls and scatter the bacon croutons over to serve, if desired.

CLAM CHOWDER

This might look a bit more complicated than the other recipes in this chapter, but it really takes no time at all. If you can't get hold of fresh clams, use a jar of clams and rinse them well in cold water before adding to the soup.

36 fresh clams, scrubbed and well rinsed
2 tablespoons sunflower oil
4 ounces ½-inch-thick slices slab bacon
4 small leeks, thinly sliced
2 celery sticks, sliced

2 potatoes, diced
3¾ cups fish stock
1 can (14-oz.) crushed tomatoes
Salt and freshly ground black pepper
2 heaping tablespoons chopped fresh parsley

Discard any cracked or opened clams that do not close when tapped; set aside the remaining clams.

Heat the oil in a large saucepan. Add the bacon and cook for about 5 minutes until crisp. Add the leeks, celery, and potatoes and cook for another 5 minutes, or so until soft.

Meanwhile, place ⅔ cup of the stock in a separate saucepan. Add the clams, cover, and cook over high heat for 3 to 4 minutes, shaking the pan occasionally, until all the clams are open; discard any that don't open.

Drain the clams, reserving the cooking liquid. Leave to cool a little, then remove the clams from most of the shells, reserving the nicest looking ones for a garnish, if desired.

Add the tomatoes to the vegetable mixture, pour in the remaining stock, and strain in the reserved clam cooking liquid through a double layer of cheesecloth to remove any sand or grit.

Season to taste and bring to a boil. Lower the heat and simmer for 8 to 10 minutes longer until the potatoes are tender but still holding their shape. Stir in the clams and parsley and heat through. Ladle into bowls and garnish with the whole reserved clams to serve, if desired.

Right: Pea and Mint Soup

SUBSTANTIAL & FILLING

This is the chapter with the soups that are a meal in themselves. Many can simmer away on the back burner for hours,

which simply helps to improve their flavors. They are also great for parties when you have to cater for

large numbers—just scale up the recipe to the quantity you need to feed. All recipes serve 4 to 6.

CAWL

This British soup takes a bit of time to make, but it's worth it—
I promise!

2¼ pounds lamb chops, each about 2 inches thick	1½ pounds potatoes, cut into large chunks
2 onions, sliced	5 cups chicken stock or water
4 small leeks, sliced	1 teaspoon fresh thyme leaves
6 carrots, sliced	1 tablespoon each softened butter and all-purpose flour
1 small rutabaga, chopped	1 tablespoon each chopped fresh flat-leaf parsley and chives
Salt and freshly ground black pepper	

Trim all the excess fat off the lamb and then render it down over low heat in a large, deep pot with a tight-fitting lid. Discard the rendered-down pieces, leaving a layer of the melted fat behind. Toss the lamb chops into the pot and cook until light brown, turning occasionally; transfer to a plate. Quickly toss the onions and leeks into the fat and then the carrots and rutabaga.

Drain any excess fat out of the pot. Layer the lamb, onions and leeks, and carrots and rutabaga, seasoning each layer. Lay the potatoes on top, so they steam while everything cooks. Pour in the stock or water, season to taste, and add the thyme. Bring to a boil. Press a circle of buttered parchment paper down on top of the potatoes and cover with a lid. Lower the heat and simmer for 1½ to 2 hours until the lamb is cooked.

When the cawl is cooked, carefully pour the cooking liquid into another saucepan. Skim off the grease and reheat the liquid.

Melt the butter in a small saucepan. Stir in the flour and cook for 1 to 2 minutes over low heat, stirring. Whisk into the liquid a little at a time until you have achieved the desired consistency. Season to taste and add the parsley and chives. Pour the liquid back into the pan with the lamb and potatoes and bring back to boiling point. Ladle into wide-rimmed bowls to serve.

SPICED BLACK BEAN SOUP

If you prefer a smooth soup, simply blend all the ingredients together just before serving, adding a little extra stock if necessary to get the desired consistency.

2 large red bell peppers	3¾ cups vegetable stock
2 tablespoons olive oil	Salt and freshly ground black pepper
1 large onion, minced	Good handful fresh cilantro leaves
2 large garlic cloves, crushed	Juice of 1 lime
2 red Scotch bonnet chilies, seeded and chopped	Sour cream cooler (page 16), to garnish (optional)
½ teaspoon each ground coriander and cumin	
2 (14-oz.) cans black beans, drained and rinsed	

Heat the broiler. Place the peppers on the broiler rack and broil for 20 to 30 minutes until charred and blistered, turning regularly. Place in a plastic bag, secure with a knot, and leave to steam in their own heat for 10 minutes. Remove from the bag and peel, seed, and dice the flesh, reserving any juices.

Meanwhile, heat the oil in a large saucepan. Add the onion, garlic, and chilies and cook for about 5 minutes until soft. Stir in the ground coriander and cumin and cook for another minute or so, stirring.

Add the beans and stock to the saucepan. Season generously and bring to a boil. Reduce the heat and simmer for 10 minutes, or until the beans are tender and heated through.

Place half of the soup in a food processor with the fresh cilantro and process to a smooth purée. Return to the pan with the diced red peppers and any of their juices. Heat through and stir in the lime juice. Season to taste. Ladle into bowls and add a spoonful of the soured cream cooler and a good grind of black pepper to serve.

SEAFOOD CHOWDER

You can also add a small diced parsnip and carrot to this soup for variety. Don't be alarmed by the addition of the Chinese five-spice powder, the flavor really does work!

6 tablespoons unsalted butter	1 onion, minced
2 carrots, diced	12 ounces firm white fish fillets, skinned and
1 potato, peeled and diced	any bones removed
2 celery sticks, diced, plus some chopped	2/3 cup fish stock
leaves, to garnish	4 ounces large cooked and shelled shrimp
1/3 cup all-purpose flour	2/3 cup heavy cream
3 3/4 cups milk	Pinch of Chinese five-spice powder
Salt and freshly ground black pepper	

Melt 2 tablespoons of the butter in a large saucepan. Add the carrots, potato, and celery, stirring to coat in the butter. Cover and cook slowly for 15 minutes until tender, stirring once or twice.

Meanwhile, melt the remaining butter in a saucepan. Remove from the heat and stir in the flour. Return to the heat and cook for 1 to 2 minutes, stirring. Gradually pour in the milk, whisking until smooth. Bring the white sauce to a boil, lower the heat, and simmer for 2 to 3 minutes, stirring occasionally. Season to taste; set aside.

Heat the oven to 350°F. Spread the onion in a small roasting pan and arrange the fish on top. Season well and pour about 4 tablespoons of the fish stock over. Cover loosely with foil and bake for 10 minutes until just opaque. Leave to cool a little, then lift the fish off the onion mixture and break into bite-sized pieces; set aside. Reserve the onion mixture.

Add the white sauce, onion mixture, and the remaining fish stock to the vegetables and slowly bring to a boil, stirring to combine. Lower the heat, carefully fold in the fish and shrimp and simmer for 1 to 2 minutes. Stir in the cream and Chinese five-spice powder and just heat through; do not boil. Season to taste. Ladle into bowls and garnish with celery leaves to serve.

CARIBBEAN SPLIT PEA SOUP

I have used canned yellow split peas in this recipe to speed up the cooking time. However, if you want, replace them with dried peas—just soak a generous 3/4 cup in plenty of water overnight and cook according to the package directions, which usually takes 1 1/2 to 2 hours.

2 tablespoons sunflower oil	3 3/4 cups vegetable stock
1 onion, minced	1 3/4 cups coconut milk
2 large garlic cloves, minced	2 cans (14-oz.) yellow split peas,
2 red Scotch bonnet chilies, seeded	drained
and minced	Pinch light brown sugar
1 teaspoon fresh thyme leaves	Salt and freshly ground black pepper
2 teaspoons medium curry powder	Tropical salsa, to garnish (page 12)
1 tablespoon paprika	

Heat the oil in a large saucepan. Add the onion, garlic, chilies, and thyme and cook slowly for 10 minutes until soft but not colored. Stir in the curry powder and paprika and cook for another minute or so, stirring.

Pour in the stock, coconut milk, split peas, and sugar. Season generously and bring to a boil. Lower the heat, cover, and simmer for 15 to 20 minutes until the split peas are soft. Season to taste and ladle into bowls. Scatter some of the tropical salsa on top to serve.

CHICKEN GUMBO

Scotch bonnets are the hottest chilies in the world, so take care when preparing them. I often rub my hands in a little oil first, which helps prevent the heat penetrating into the skin.

3 tablespoons olive oil	2 green Scotch bonnet chilies, seeded and
1 large onion, minced	minced
4 celery sticks, minced	5 cups chicken stock
1 green bell pepper, seeded and minced	1 can (14-oz) crushed tomatoes in rich
1 1/2 cups fresh okra, cut into 1/4-inch	tomato juice
slices	1 bouquet garni
1 pound boneless and skinless chicken	4 ounces chorizo or kielbasa sausages,
thighs, quartered	casings removed and sliced
2 tablespoons seasoned all-purpose flour	Salt and freshly ground black pepper
2 garlic cloves, minced	

Heat the oil in a large saucepan. Add the onion, celery, green pepper, and okra and cook slowly for 10 to 15 minutes until the vegetables are tender but not colored. Toss the chicken in the flour until well coated. Push the vegetables to one side of the pan and add the chicken. Stir-fry for a few minutes until the chicken is sealed and just golden.

Add the garlic and chilies to the pan and cook for 1 to 2 minutes longer, stirring until everything is combined. Pour in the stock and add the tomatoes, bouquet garni, and sausages. Season to taste and bring to a boil. Lower the heat and simmer for 25 to 30 minutes until the soup is reduced and thicker. Ladle into bowls to serve.

Right: Seafood Chowder

Above: Pumpkin and Melted Onion Soup

MOROCCAN HARIRA SOUP

Muslims traditionally sit down to enjoy a soup like this at the end of the day during the holy month of Ramadan, when not a bite of food can be consumed between sunrise and sunset. No wonder they need something so nourishing!

1 small cinnamon stick	3³/4 cups chicken stock
4 whole cloves	1 can (14-oz.) crushed tomatoes
1 teaspoon each mustard, cumin, and	1 can (14-oz.) garbanzo beans, rinsed
coriander seeds	About 3 tablespoons harissa (hot chili
2 tablespoons olive oil	paste)
1 onion, chopped	Salt and freshly ground black pepper
12 ounces boneless lamb meat, such as	1 tablespoon each chopped fresh cilantro and
tenderloin, cut into bite-size pieces	flat-leaf parsley
1 tablespoon all-purpose flour	Juice of ¹/2 lemon

Warm a small skillet. Add the cinnamon stick, cloves, and mustard, cumin, and coriander seeds. Toast for 1 to 2 minutes until aromatic and lightly darker in color, tossing occasionally. Place the spices in a spice blender or use a mortar and pestle and crush to a powder.

Heat the oil in a deep skillet. Add the onion and cook for 2 to 3 minutes until soft. Add the lamb and cook for a few minutes until sealed. Tip in the spices and flour, stirring to combine. Cook for a minute or so. Pour in the stock, add the tomatoes, and simmer for 15 to 20 minutes until the lamb is completely tender.

Add the garbanzo beans and enough harissa to suit your taste and stir well. Season to taste and cook for few minutes until heated through. Stir in the herbs and lemon juice and ladle into bowls to serve.

CALDO VERDE

Normally made with a member of the cabbage family called *couve gallego*, this is Portugal's national dish. Curly kale is the nearest green to it that is readily available, but really any type of cabbage will do.

4 tablespoons olive oil, plus extra, to garnish	7 ounces chorizo sausages, casings removed
1 large Spanish onion, halved and	and sliced
thinly sliced	5 cups chicken stock
1 large red bell pepper, seeded and sliced	12 ounces baby new potatoes, halved
1 large yellow bell pepper, seeded and	Salt and freshly ground black pepper
thinly sliced	6¹/2 cups cored and finely shredded curly
2 garlic cloves, crushed	kale or other cabbage

Heat the oil in a large saucean. Add the onion, peppers, and garlic and cook for about 10 minutes until the peppers are soft and beginning to caramelize. Stir in the chorizo and cook for another few minutes until sizzling, stirring occasionally. Pour in the stock and add the potatoes. Season generously and bring to a boil. Lower the heat, cover, and simmer for 15 to 20 minutes until the potatoes are tender.

Stir the curly kale into the pan, cover, and cook for 3 to 4 minutes longer until wilted and tender. Season to taste and ladle into bowls. Add swirls of olive oil and serve hot.

PUMPKIN AND MELTED ONION SOUP

For an even richer version, stir in 1 cup diced cheese, such as Gruyère or fontina, just before serving. It's a match made in heaven!

2¹/4 pounds pumpkin or butternut squash	2 teaspoons chopped fresh sage
3 tablespoons olive oil	2 garlic cloves, minced
Salt and freshly ground black pepper	3³/4 cups vegetable or chicken stock
2 tablespoons unsalted butter	³/4 cup crème fraîche or sour cream
2 large onions, minced	Parmesan croutons (page 14), to garnish

Preheat the oven to 475°F. Cut the pumpkin or squash into wedges, no more than 3 inches, and scoop out the seeds. Brush all over with 1 tablespoon of the oil and place on a roasting tray. Season generously and roast near the top of the oven for 45 minutes, or until caramelized. Leave until cool enough to handle, then scrape the flesh away from the skin; you should have about 1 pound, or about 2 cups.

Heat the remaining oil in a large saucepan with the butter. Add the onions and cook for 25 minutes until brown, stirring frequently. Add the sage and garlic and cook for 5 minutes. Add the pumpkin and stock and simmer for 15 to 20 minutes until the pumpkin is tender.

Purée the soup in batches in a food processor or with a hand-held mixer. Return to the saucepan. Add most of the crème fraîche, season to taste, and reheat slowly. Ladle into bowls and top with spoonfuls of crème fraîche or sour cream and the Parmesan croutons to serve.

CREAMY SALMON TARRAGON SOUP

This is so rich and tasty that it really is a meal in itself. I love to eat this with star-shaped pastry puffs floating on the top. Obviously you can use any cut of salmon but the fillets save a lot of time because they cook so quickly.

1 tablespoons sunflower oil
2 tablespoons unsalted butter
Four 4-ounce salmon fillets
Salt and freshly ground black pepper
2 large shallots, minced
1 small garlic clove, crushed
2½ cups sliced button mushrooms
2 tablespoons all-purpose flour

1 cup dry white wine
3¾ cups fish stock
2 zucchini, halved and sliced on the
    diagonal
⅔ cups heavy cream
2 tablespoons minced fresh tarragon
Pastry puffs (page 14), to garnish,
    (optional)

Heat the oil with the butter in a large saucepan. Season the salmon all over and add to the saucepan. Sear for 1 to 2 minutes on each side until lightly golden and just tender. Transfer to a plate and leave to cool a little; roughly flake into smaller pieces.

Stir the shallots into the saucepan and cook for about 5 minutes until soft. Add the garlic and mushrooms, stirring until well coated. Season and stir-fry for a few minutes until the mushrooms are tender. Stir in the flour and cook for another minute or so, stirring constantly.

Pour the wine into the saucepan and boil rapidly for a few minutes, scraping the base with a wooden spoon. Pour in the stock and simmer for 25 to 30 minutes until lightly thickened and reduced.

Stir in the zucchini and cream. Continue simmering for 2 to 3 minutes until the zucchini are just tender and the cream has slightly reduced. Return the salmon to the saucepan with the tarragon and just warm through. Season to taste and ladle into bowls. Garnish with the pastry shapes, if desired, to serve.

CARIBBEAN CRAB CALLALOO

Callaloo is a generic name given to the green leafy tops of the taro and malanga plants. If you can't get hold of it fresh, you can buy it in cans from West Indian grocers. Spinach is a good substitute.

2 tablespoons unsalted butter
1 tablespoon sunflower oil
4 ounces ½-inch-thick slices slab bacon
1 large onion, minced
1 red Scotch bonnet chili, seeded
    and minced
2 garlic cloves, crushed
2 cups diced potatoes

1 teaspoon fresh thyme leaves
3¾ cups chicken or vegetable stock
1¾ cups coconut milk
3 cups finely shredded callaloo
2 cups fresh or canned white crabmeat
Few drops hot-pepper sauce
Salt and freshly ground black pepper

Melt the butter in a large saucepan with the oil. Add the bacon and cook for about 5 minutes until crisp. Add the onion, chili, and garlic and cook slowly for another 5 minutes until soft but not colored.

Add the potatoes to the pan with the thyme, stock, and coconut milk and bring to a boil. Lower the heat and simmer for 10 to 15 minutes until the potatoes are tender.

Stir in the callaloo and cook for a few minutes, stirring occasionally until just beginning to wilt. Stir in the crabmeat and hot-pepper sauce and season to taste. Simmer for a few minutes until the crab is heated through but the callaloo is still green. Ladle into bowls to serve.

MINESTRONE SOUP

You can use any type of small pasta shapes for this recipe, or just snap dried macaroni, spaghetti, or tagliatelle into small pieces.

2 tablespoons olive oil
4 ounces ½-inch-thick slices slab bacon
2 small leeks, minced
2 carrots, minced
2 celery sticks, finely sliced
2 garlic cloves, minced
1 teaspoon fresh thyme leaves
3¾ cups vegetable stock
1 can (14-oz.) crushed tomatoes

1 heaping tablespoon sun-dried tomato paste
½ cup small dried pasta shapes, such as
    broken macaroni
Salt and freshly ground black pepper
4 savoy cabbage leaves, thick stems
    removed and leaves shredded
1 small zucchini, thinly sliced
6 tablespoons pesto (page 12)
4 to 6 ciabatta croûtes (page 14)

Heat the oil in a large saucepan. Add the bacon and cook for 5 minutes until golden. Add the leeks, carrots, and celery and cook slowly for about 5 minutes until soft but not brown. Add the garlic and thyme and cook for 2 to 3 minutes longer without coloring. Stir in the stock, the tomatoes, and sun-dried tomato paste, and bring to a boil. Add the pasta, season to taste, cover, and simmer for 10 minutes, or until *al dente*.

Heat the broiler. Stir the cabbage into the soup and cook for a minute or so until just wilted. Add the zucchini and cook for another minute until just tender. Stir in a heaping tablespoon of the pesto and season to taste. Ladle the soup into flameproof serving bowls. Spread the croûtes with the remaining pesto and arrange on top of the soup. Place under the broiler until the pesto is bubbling. Serve at once.

FRENCH ONION SOUP

Hard cider instead of beer gives this classic French bistro soup a more subtle, mellow flavor. Use any type of Swiss cheese, or try an equal mixture of Gruyère and Parmesan cheeses, which also works well.

1 tablespoon olive oil
2 tablespoons unsalted butter
2½ cups thinly sliced onions
½ teaspoon salt
Good pinch of sugar
3¾ cups chicken stock

2 tablespoons all-purpose flour
¾ cup good-quality hard cider
Salt and freshly ground black pepper
2 tablespoons Cognac or other brandy
12 to 18 croutes (page 14)
½ cup finely grated Gruyère cheese

Heat the oil with the butter in a large, heavy-bottomed saucepan. Add the onions, cover, and cook slowly for 15 minutes, stirring occasionally. Uncover, increase the heat, and stir in the salt and the sugar. Continue to cook for 45 minutes longer, stirring frequently so the onions do not stick as they caramelize.

When the onions are a deep golden color, pour the stock into another saucepan and bring to a simmer. Stir the flour into the onions and cook for 1 to 2 minutes, stirring. Gradually add the cider to the onions, stirring continuously, and then pour in the boiling stock, stirring to prevent any lumps from forming. Bring to a boil. Lower the heat, cover, and simmer for about 30 minutes until the onions are meltingly tender and the soup has thickened. Season to taste.

Just before serving, preheat the broiler. Stir the Cognac or brandy into the soup and ladle into flameproof serving bowls. Float the croûtes on top and sprinkle the Gruyère over. Place under the broiler until the cheese melts and bubbles. Serve at once.

CULLEN SKINK

Make this very traditional Scottish soup and you'll see why its popularity has stood the test of time. I strongly recommend you use undyed smoked haddock for the best flavor and color, rather than the bright yellow stuff.

2½ cups floury potatoes, cut into small
  chunks
4 tablespoons unsalted butter
Salt and freshly ground black pepper
1 large onion, chopped
1 pound natural smoked haddock,
  cut into large pieces

2 cups water
1¼ cups fish or chicken stock
1¼ cups milk
1 heaping tablespoon snipped fresh chives
⅔ cup heavy cream

Place the potatoes in a pan of boiling, salted water, cover, and simmer for 15 to 20 minutes until tender. Drain and mash well. Beat in half the butter and season to taste. Set aside.

Melt the remaining butter in a large saucepan. Add the onion and cook slowly for about 5 minutes until soft but not colored. Add the haddock and pour the water on top. Simmer for 10 minutes until the fish is just cooked through and flakes easily.

Lift out the pieces of fish with a draining spoon. Transfer to a plate and leave until cool enough to handle; roughly flake, discarding any skin and bones.

Stir the mashed potato into the cooking liquid, mixing until combined. Pour in the stock and milk and bring to a boil. Quickly lower the heat and simmer for 3 to 4 minutes until heated through and combined, stirring occasionally.

Stir the flaked fish, chives, and cream into the pan and cook slowly for a few minutes until heated through. Season to taste. Ladle into bowls and serve at once.

Right: *French Onion Soup*

HUNGARIAN GOULASH SOUP

If you don't want to use pork tenderloin, beef or chicken work just as well. For a vegetarian version, simply replace the meat with one (14-oz.) can mixed beans that have been drained and rinsed.

2 tablespoons sunflower oil	1 tablespoon seasoned all-purpose flour
1 red onion, chopped	3³/4 cups chicken or vegetable stock
2 red bell peppers, seeded and minced	1 can (14-oz.) crushed tomatoes
1 large garlic clove, crushed	1 heaping tablespoon tomato paste
1¹/2 cups sliced mushrooms	Salt and freshly ground black pepper
12 ounces pork tenderloin, cut in small strips	4 ounces dried pasta bows (farfalle)
1 heaping tablespoon hot paprika, plus extra for dusting	Sour cream and chopped fresh flat-leaf parsley, to garnish

Heat the oil in a large saucepan. Stir in the onion and peppers and cook for 2 to 3 minutes until soft. Stir in the garlic and mushrooms and cook over high heat for a few minutes until the mushrooms are tender.

Meanwhile, toss the pork strips in the paprika and seasoned flour until coated. Push the mushroom mixture to the side of the pan and add the pork. Stir-fry for a few minutes until just tender and light brown.

Pour the stock into the pan. Add the tomatoes and tomato paste. Season to taste and bring to a boil. Lower the heat, stir in the pasta bows, and simmer for 10 to 15 minutes longer until the pasta is *al dente*. Ladle into bowls and garnish with a swirl of sour cream, a dusting of paprika, and a sprinkling of parsley to serve.

WINTER LENTIL AND VEGETABLE SOUP

This soup certainly won't break the bank. Don't be afraid to leave out a vegetable if you don't have it on hand, or to substitute one for another.

2 tablespoons olive oil	4 large, ripe tomatoes, peeled and roughly chopped
4 ounces ¹/2-inch-thick slices slab bacon	
1 large onion, minced	¹/2 cup red lentils
2 small leeks, thinly sliced	1 bouquet garni
2 carrots, chopped	Salt and freshly ground black pepper
2 celery sticks, chopped	Juice of ¹/2 lemon
2 garlic cloves, minced	2 heaping tablespoons roughly chopped fresh flat-leaf parsley
5 cups vegetable stock	

Heat the oil in a large saucepan. Add the bacon and cook for about 5 minutes until crisp. Push it to one side of the pan, add the onion and leeks and cook slowly for a few minutes until soft. Stir in the carrots, celery, and garlic and cook for another 4 to 5 minutes, stirring occasionally, without letting the vegetables color.

Pour the stock into the saucepan. Add the tomatoes, lentils, and bouquet garni and bring to a boil. Lower the heat, cover, and simmer for 30 minutes, or until the lentils are tender. Season to taste and stir in the lemon juice and parsley. Ladle into bowls and serve at once.

PEA AND HAM SOUP

For a real treat, use the freshest of peas and new potatoes and all you'll need is a hunk of moist, crusty bread for a complete meal.

4 tablespoons unsalted butter	2 cups cooked smoked ham, cut into small dice
1 onion, minced	
¹/2 pound new potatoes, scrubbed and diced	²/3 cup heavy cream
2¹/2 cups fresh or frozen peas	1 egg yolk
3³/4 cups chicken stock	1 tablespoon each chopped fresh flat-leaf parsley and mint
Salt and freshly ground black pepper	

Melt the butter in a large saucepan. Add the onion and potatoes and cook slowly for about 10 minutes until the potatoes are almost tender but not colored.

Stir the peas and stock into the pan and season to taste. Bring to the boil. Lower the heat and simmer for 4 to 5 minutes until the peas are tender. Leave to cool a little.

Roughly purée in a food processor or with a hand-held blender and pour back into a clean saucepan. Stir in the ham and reheat slowly.

Mix together the cream, egg yolk, and herbs in a bowl and whisk in a ladleful of the hot soup. Whisk into the soup and simmer for 3 to 4 minutes longer until warmed through, stirring occasionally; do not boil. Season to taste and ladle into bowls. Serve at once.

TUSCAN BEAN SOUP

This soup is especially delicious when made with really sweet, ripe, juicy tomatoes. If it is not the right time of the year for them, replace with two (14-oz.) cans crushed tomatoes.

³/4 cup dried cannellini beans, soaked overnight	1 heaping tablespoon chopped fresh oregano
	Good pinch of sugar
4 tablespoons extra-virgin olive oil	Salt and freshly ground black pepper
2 large garlic cloves, minced	2¹/2 cups vegetable or chicken stock
2¹/2 pounds plum tomatoes, peeled, seeded, and diced	2 tablespoons shredded fresh basil
	4 to 6 tablespoons pesto (page 12)

Place the beans in a large pan and cover with water. Slowly bring to the boil and boil vigorously for 10 minutes. Lower the heat and simmer for about 1 hour until the beans are soft but still holding their shape. Drain and rinse under cold water. Set aside.

Heat the oil in a large, heavy-bottomed saucepan. Add the garlic and cook over low heat for 2 to 3 minutes, being careful not to let it brown. Add the tomatoes, oregano, and sugar, season to taste, and bring to a boil. Lower the heat and simmer for about 15 minutes until thick.

Pour in the stock and season to taste. Return to a boil. Lower the heat and simmer for 15 to 20 minutes longer until the tomatoes are thoroughly combined and the soup has thickened. Stir in the cooked beans and basil and heat through. Ladle into bowls, add a swirl of pesto to each one and serve at once.

Right: Tuscan Bean Soup

RECIPE INDEX

ACKNOWLEDGMENTS

This book is dedicated to Derek, for all his help, patience, and support. With special thanks to my mum for all the time spent cleaning up after my recipe testing sessions. Particular thanks to Debbie Major, who gave the manuscript a final read and offered invaluable comments. Thanks also to Laura Washburn and Maggie Ramsay at Weidenfeld & Nicolson and to Emma Patmore for her great food styling. Also, to all the food writers and chefs who have inspired me over the years. Lastly, a big thank you to Mitzie Wilson, my first boss at *BBC Good Food* magazine, for believing in me and sending me on my way.

First published in the United States of America
in 1999 by
Rizzoli International Publications, Inc.
300 Park Avenue South
New York, NY 10010

First published in 1999 by
Weidenfeld and Nicolson
Illustrated Division
The Orion Publishing Group
Wellington House
125 Strand
London WC2R 0BB

Text copyright © Weidenfeld & Nicolson 1999
Photographs © Robin Matthews

ISBN 0-8478-2205-2
LC 99-70291

Stylist: Roisin Nield
Home economist: Emma Patmore

Printed in Italy by Printer Trento srl.